Unorganized retail from the lens of customers : A case study of Kolhapur City

Dr. Hemlata Vivek Gaikwad
M.Sc , MBA , M.Phil , Ph.D
Asst. Professor Rajarambapu Institute of Technology, Islampur, Sangli, Maharshtra

UnOrganized retail from the lens of customers :
A case study of Kolhapur City

Dr. Hemlata Vivek Gaikwad
M.Sc , MBA , M.Phil , Ph.D
Asst. Professor
Rajarambapu Institute of Technology, Islampur,
Sangli, Maharshtra

Preface

The Indian history shows that unorganized retail is the core of India . Before anybody knew about what retail is, we had kirana stores, medical stores and lot many other stores working surprisingly well all over the country. But the entry of the big organized retail giants brought a question of the existence of the unorganized retail sector. The growth in the Indian organized retail market is mainly due to the change in the consumer's behaviour. This change has come in the consumer due to increased income, changing lifestyles, and patterns of demography which are favourable. This generated an urgent need of understanding the unorganized retail being in the shoes of a consumer.

The present book provides the insight on the unorganized retail from the lens of the customer. Kolhapur city of Maharashtra was taken for the study as it is a very big city with both organized and unorganized retail players. Thus the insight given by these customers will be very useful in developing strategies for future .

Author also invite valuable suggestions / criticism for further improvement from readers.

Contents

Preface

1. INTRODUCTION TO THE RETAIL SCENARIO IN INDIA   5-14
1 Introduction
2 Global Scenario of Retailing
3 Indian Scenario of Retailing
4 Recent Past History of Organized Indian Retail
5 Challenges
6 Emerging Retail Formats
7 Overview of the book

2. OPINION OF GLOBAL EXPERTS   15 - 31
1 Introduction
2 Review Of Books At International Scenario
3 Review Of Ph.D. Thesis
4 Review Of Research Papers
5 Concluding Remarks

3. THEORETICAL CONCEPT OF MARKETING   32- 50
1. Introduction
2. Marketing
3. The Marketing Mix
4. Marketing strategies
5. Retail Operations

4. PROFILE OF KOLHAPUR DISTRICT   51 - 62
1 Introduction
2 History of Kolhapur City
3 District Profile

5. CUSTOMER'S OPINION ON UNORGANIZED RETAIL   63 - 144
1 Introduction
2. Findings from the customer's lens
3 Findings for Shopkeepers
4. Suggestions for Customers
5. Suggestions for Shopkeepers
6. Implications for Consumers
7 Implications for Retailers
8. Recommendations for Future Research
9. Conclusion

References

Chapter I
INTRODUCTION TO THE RETAIL SCENARIO IN INDIA

1 Introduction

Retailing encompasses the business activities involving goods and services to their consumers for their personal family / household use. Retailing is the largest private industry in the world with total sales of US $ 6.6 trillion. The retail sectors play a significant role in the world economy because of the contribution that it makes to the economy of the country.

Retail, according to concise Oxford English Dictionary, is the 'sale of goods to the public for use or consumption rather than for resale'. Retailing is derived from the French word 'retailer' meaning 'breaking bulk', specifically, breaking bulk quantities into smaller saleable units. Usually, a retailer buys goods or products in larger quantities from manufacturers or importers, either directly or through a wholesaler and then sells individual items in small quantities to general public or the end users. As such, retailing is the last link that connects the individual consumer with the manufacturing and distribution chain.

The world over retail sector has been growing rapidly with increasing sophistication and modernization of the life-style of households and individuals and also with increasing globalization of trade. The retail sector has strong backward and forward linkages with other sectors like agriculture and industry through stimulating demand for goods and through mass marketing, packaging, storage and transport. Moreover, it creates considerable direct and indirect employment in the economy. Also, the consumers have benefited in terms of wide range of products available in a market.

The retail industry in India is of late often being hailed as one of the sunrise sectors in the economy. A.T. Kearney, the well known international management consultant, recently identified India as the second most attractive retail destination globally from among thirty emergent markets.

The Retail sectors have become one of the most dynamic growing sectors in recent times. Retailing has always been an integral part of economic development. Nations with strong retail activity have enjoyed greater economic and social progress. It contributes to the development by matching the individual requirements of the population with the producers and suppliers of merchandise. By bringing the product to the customers, they are helpful in creation of demand of new offers leading to expansion of market. The Indian retail industry is not only one of the most fragmented in the world, but also the most challenging due to its unorganized nature.

The retail sector is broadly classified in to two groups; organized and unorganized retail sector. The organized retailing refers to trading activities undertaken by licensed retailers, that is, those who are registered for sale tax, income tax, etc. These include the corporate – backed hypermarkets and retail chains, and also privately owned large retail businesses. It is not just stocking and selling but is more about efficient supply chain management, developing vendor relationships, quality customer service, efficient merchandising and timely promotional campaigns. On the other hand the unorganized retailing refers to the traditional formats of low-cost retailing, for example, the local kirana shops, owner managed general stores, convenience stores, hand cart and pavement vendors, etc. This market is characterized by typically small retailers, more prone to tax evasion and lack of labour law supervision. This market is more common in developing countries.

2 Global Scenario of Retailing

Retail has played a major role world over in increasing their activity across a wide range of consumer goods and services. The impact can be seen in countries like U.S.A., U.K., Mexico, Thailand and more recently China. Economies of countries like Singapore, Malaysia, Hong Kong, Sri Lanka and Dubai are also heavily assisted by the retail sector.

Globally, retailing is a big business and its turnover accounts to US $ 6.6 trillion. The retail industry in America employs more than 22 million people and generates more than US$ 3.0 trillion in retail sale annually (*www.epwrf.res.in*). According to the India retail report 2005, the retail sales was found to be the highest in developed countries like U.S.A. and U.K., wherein 85 per cent of the retail sector was constituted by organized retailing due to 100 per cent foreign direct investment (FDI) and its contribution of nine per cent to GDP and more than 10 per cent employment in these countries (www.imagesretail.com/ india_retail_report.htm). The share of organized retail is more so in case of developed countries due to the busy life schedule and lack of time for shopping for the common man, high literacy rate, exposure to media, greater availability and penetration of variety of consumer goods into the interiors of the country and better shopping experience. Whereas, the share of organized retail outlets in developing countries was very less, it was 17 per cent in China and very meagre, about Three per cent, in India because of the poor literacy rate, lack of exposure to media, non-availability and low penetration of consumer goods to rural areas of the country and lack of shopping experiences.

There are many Multi National Companies (MNCs) operating in the retail business throughout the world. The big four champions in 2004 were Wal-Mart, Carrefour, Home Depot and Target. Except Carrefour, which hailed from France, all three top champions were from U.S.A. The combined sales was US $ 438 billion and were growing at the rate of 10 per cent per annum, there growth came from putting small stores out of business. This is happening in Europe and Asia also in recent times. The Big Box and Hypermarket are operating everywhere. However, Germany based Metro is operating in 27 countries all over the world including India.

3 Indian Scenario of Retailing

Retailing is one of the largest industry in India and second largest employer after agriculture. The retailing industry provides employment to over 18 million people. One out of every 25 families in India is engaged in the business of retailing. Ownership and management are predominantly family controlled. However, in sharp contrast to developed countries, unit average size of retail outlet in India is very small. It is the Tenth largest economy in the world based on GDP. The Indian retail sector is growing at compound average growth rate (CAGR) of 30 per cent over the last five years. However, the share of modern organized retail sector is likely to grow from its current Three percent to 15-20 per cent over the next decade. More than Eight per cent of the population is engaged in this activity. The Indian retail industry is valued at US $300 billion and is expected to grow to US $637 billion by the end of 2015. The retail sector was expected to generate employment in excess of 20 lakhs by 2010 of which 5-6 lakhs is in the organized sector. The country is rated as fifth most attractive emerging retail sector and ranked second in a Global Retail Development Index of 30 developing countries as drawn up by A.T. Kearney.

Unlike most other countries, Indian retail sector is highly fragmented and bulk of the business is in the unorganized sector (97 per cent) like local 'wet' market vendors, roadside pushcart sellers or tiny kirana (grocery) stores. In India, the majority of food consumption is still at home. There are an estimated 12 million retail outlets, of which almost Seven million sell food and grocery products. The vast majority of these are small kiosks (17 per cent), general provision stores (14 per cent) and grocery stores (called kirana; 56 per cent of all rural retail outlets) run by a single trader and his family. With more than 71 per cent of the population living in small villages and engaged in agriculture, most of Indians still do their food shopping at small-scale vendors in the local village, or at large-scale weekly markets which are often serving several villages in one area, where small individual vendors trade. In the towns and cities, most consumers do their food shopping at the local neighbourhood, independent small retailers, kiosks and street hawkers. (Anonymous, 2005).

Organized retailing accounts for only Three per cent in India, whereas it is 85 per cent in USA and U.K., 75 percent in Taiwan, 55 percent in Malaysia, 35 per cent in Korea and 20 per cent in China. The growth of retail sector in the country is tremendous, both in urban and rural areas. The country has witnessed a retail revolution in recent years. Significant development has been taking place in urban areas in the form of organized retailing, mega stores or malls, more so in the south of the country in the major cities of Bangalore, Chennai and Hyderabad, as well as New Delhi and Mumbai in the North. It is expected that the Tier II cities would take another five years to absorb modern retailing opportunities. Moreover, the case for Indian retailers to explore rural markets is also strong due to the size of rural population and agricultural income growth in last couple of years. The major formats being followed for organized food retailing in India are supermarkets, discount stores, fresh product outlets, specialty stores, convenience stores and off price retailers.

International attention is now increasingly focused on the rapidly growing Indian food retail market. With the removal of quantitative restrictions on imports, Indian consumers can have access to food from around the world. Market analysts believe that hypermarket will determine the future of organized food retailing over the short to medium term. Traditional grocers are also gradually redefining themselves by increasing floor space and introducing self-service format and value added services such as credit and home delivery (Anonymous, 2004).

Food retailing is one of the important part of the present organized retail industry in the world. Growing at a rate of 30 per cent, the Indian food retail is going to be a major driving force for the retail industry. The changing life styles, tastes and higher disposable income, growing need for convenience, etc. has revolutionalized the food retail scenario of the country and now it has become the largest segment of the retail sector of India.

4 Recent Past History of Organized Indian Retail

Till 2008 the Indian Organized Retail Industry was growing at a breakneck speed. It was widely said that the 90s belonged to the IT industry whereas the 2000s belonged to the Retail Industry. By 2005 the Industry had become a $350 Billion business (Source: ICRIER Report 2005) and all the Industry players had gigantic plans for investment.

Table 1.1 : Investment Figures of Companies (2006)

Company	Investment
Wal-Mart	Yet to announce
Reliance	$5.5 Billion
Aditya Birla	$3.3 Billion
Pantaloon	$1 Billion
Tatas	$89 Million

Source: The Economic times

The Growth of the industry was driven by the following factors:

1. Young Population: India's young participation is very very young. Also most of them are getting their jobs at a very early age. This generation is mostly a post liberalization generation. They have grown up seeing the advent of the global brands in India, internet and the television.

2. Higher Income of Consumers: The higher income of the consumers proved to be a great factor of growth for the Retail industry. The Retail Industry depends on the income of the consumers. That's why when income of the customers is good its bound to benefit the retailers.

3. No Money, No Problem: with the liberalization of the Indian Economy a boom also came for the Banking. Financial Services and Insurance (BFSI) sector which led to more and more customers started using credit cards due to the more benefits available.

4. Urbanization: More and more satellite towns have been built up all through out the country. Notable examples include Gurgaon and Noida in the North, Rajarhaat in East, Navi Mumbai in West and UB city in the South. The Satellite towns have also fuelled the growth of the retail industry.

Table 1.2 : Indian Retail Market Size

Years	Market Size (In Billion dollars)
1998	201
2000	204
2002	238
2004	278
2006	321
2008	368
2010	421
2012	450

Source : A T Kearney

Table 1.3 : Percentage of Population Living in Urban India

Years	Percentage of population
1951	17.3
1961	18
1981	23.3
1991	25.7
2001	27.8
2011	37.7

Source : A T Kearney

All the above factors led India to occupy the leading position in the Global Retail Development Index study by A T Kearney.

Table1. 4 : Segment wise Performance of the Indian Retail Sector

	Indian retail Market			Organized Retail Market		
Retail Segment	2006	2007	Growth	2006	2007	Growth
Clothing, Textiles & Fashion Accessories	113,500	1,38,300	17,800	21,400	29,800	8,400
Jewellery	60,200	69,400	9,200	1,680	2,300	620
Watches	3,950	4,400	450	1,800	2,150	350
Footwear	13,750	16,000	2,250	5,200	7,750	2,550
Health & Beauty care services	3,800	4,600	800	400	660	260
Pharmaceuticals	42,200	48,800	6,600	1,100	1,540	440

Consumer Durables, Home Appliances / equipments	48,100	57,500	9,400	5,000	7,100	2,100
Mobile handsets, Accessories & Services	21,650	27,200	5,550	1,740	2,700	960
Furnishings, Utensils, Furniture-Home & Office	40,650	45,500	4,850	3,700	5,000	1,300
Food & Grocery	7,43,900	7,92,000	48,100	5,800	9,000	3,200
Out-of-Home Food (Catering) Services	57,000	71,300	14,300	3,940	5,700	1,760
Books, Music & Gifts	13,300	16,400	3,100	1,680	2,200	520
Entertainment	38,000	45,600	7,600	1,560	2,400	840

Source : Images F & R Research

The above table shows that food & Groceries was providing the largest amount of opportunity.

Sensing this opportunity the Industrial Groups came up with their billion dollar plans. But their plans led to a very powerful uprising from the trader and middlemen class backed by State Governments all throughout the country and they had to especially Reliance closed down several stores in West Bengal and UP.

Table 1.5 : Share of Organised Retail to Total Market

Retail Segment	Organized Retail Market			
	2004	2005	2006	2007
Clothing, Textiles & Fashion Accessories	13.60%	15.80%	18.90%	22.70%
Jewellery	2.00%	2.30%	2.80%	3.30%
Watches	13.60%	43.50%	45.60%	48.90%
Footwear	25.00%	30.30%	37.80%	48.40%
Health & Beauty care services	6.00%	7.60%	10.60%	14.30%
Pharmaceuticals	1.80%	2.20%	2.60%	3.20%
Consumer Durables, Home Appliances/equipments	7.80%	8.80%	10.40%	12.30%
Mobile handsets, Accessories & Services	6.50%	7.00%	8.00%	9.90%
Furnishings, Utensils, Furniture-Home & Office	6.70%	7.60%	9.10%	11.00%

Food & Grocery	0.50%	0.60%	0.80%	1.10%
Out-of-Home Food (Catering) Services	5.70%	5.80%	6.90%	8.80%
Books, Music & Gifts	9.80%	11.70%	12.60%	13.40%
Entertainment	2.60%	3.30%	4.10%	5.30%

Source : Images F & R Research

5 Challenges

In India, insufficient work has been done on identifying the consumers' behaviour towards emerging retail format, impact of consumers' demographic profiles, attributes of emerging retail formats, product-wise consumer preferences from different retail formats and retail marketing strategies. The previous studies have covered only one or two aspects of retailing. Thus, it has become imperative to study all the important aspects of retailing together in order to know the latest trends of retailing and changing consumers' behaviour towards these trends. So the present study proposes to cover consumers' and retailers' perspective in Kolhapur. Currently, it is very important for retailers to understand the need of customers before carrying a product because of changing consumer preferences and life style. The study will also identify the consumers' behaviour towards emerging retail formats like malls, speciality stores, hyper/supermarkets, discount stores, convenience stores and department stores, impact of demographic factors on consumers' behaviour, and attributes influencing purchasing from these retail formats.

6 Emerging Retail Formats:

Emerging retail formats provide a wide variety to customers and offer an ideal shopping experience with an amalgamation of product, entertainment and service, all under a single roof. Indian retail scenario, with the intervention of organized retail in the form of modern retail formats such as one-stop malls, speciality malls, hyper markets and big-box retailing, has witnessed a remarkable shift in the preferences of consumers. According to Hino (2010) the emergence and expansion of supermarkets has gradually decreased the market share of the traditional formats. The factors that helped supermarkets gain consumer preference over the traditional stores are the 'consumers' economic ability' and the 'format output'. Kuruvilla and Ganguli (2008) opine that mall development is expected to grow at a frantic pace in metros and mini metros. Malls comprise 90% of the total future retail development. The basic reason for the growth of malls is that it offers an experience and not just goods. There is a wide range of shopping experience -bargains and discounts, high-end brands for couples, gaming and other amusement facilities for kids and the multiplexes theatres, etc. The formats considered in the present study are:

i. **Malls**: Malls ranging from 60,000 sq. ft. to 7,00,000 sq. ft, are the largest form of organized retailing today. These lend an ideal shopping experience with an amalgamation of product, service and entertainment, all under a single roof.

ii. **Convenience Stores**: These are relatively small stores located near residential areas and open for long hours for all seven days a week. These carry a limited line of high-turnover convenience products and fill important consumer needs. People are willing to pay for the convenience.

iii. **Department Stores**: Department Stores are another type of emerging formats and these carry several product lines- typically clothing, home furnishings and house-hold goods -with each line operating as a separate department managed by specialist buyers or merchandisers.

iv. **Hypermarkets/Supermarkets**: Hypermarkets and Supermarkets are the latest formats located in or near residential high streets. Hypermarkets carry a product range varying from Foods, Home-ware, Appliances, Furniture, Sports, Toys and Clothing; an Supermarkets are large self - service outlets, catering to varied shopper needs and mainly focus on Food and Grocery and personal sales.

v. **Discount Stores**: Consumers preferring to pay a low price can visit the Discount Stores or Factory Outlets, which offer discounts on the MRP, as they sell in bulk and have higher economies of scale.

vi. **Speciality Stores**: These stores especially cater to consumers who are looking for assorted brands at one store. For instance, apparel stores, sporting goods stores, furniture stores and book stores are some of the examples of speciality stores. (Kotler, 2006; Sinha,2007 and Jasola, 2007)

7 Overview of the book

The present study takes a holistic perspective of retailing. The study focuses on identifying
The consumers' behaviour towards emerging retail formats, considering the impact of demographic factors on consumers' behaviour and attributes influencing consumers to purchase from these retail formats. Also included in the study are the types of goods preferred for buying from emerging retail formats. The study takes into account the retailers' perspective as well by identifying the important retail marketing strategies influencing consumers' purchase preferences.

The study, by taking into account consumers' and retailers' perspective, tries to present a holistic picture of retail scenario.

CHAPTER II
OPINION OF GLOBAL EXPERTS

1 Introduction

At present there is a vast literature available in this field in India and around the globe. But it is surprising to note that none of the studies have focused on comparative analysis of small retail houses and Large retail houses. A few which have tried to do so are also limited to one or two aspects only. The present chapter discusses the literature available in and around the current study being undertaken.

2 Review Of Books At International Scenario

R.N. Mishra (2010)

The author in his book titles "**Marketing Strategies In Retail Sector**" says that the service sector accounts for a large share of GDF in most developed economics and the retail sector forms a very strong component of the service sector. Retail will generate employment. At present retail sector considered most important in changing the GDP of the country. It provide more than 80% of employment opportunities. The network of retailers reaches every nook and corner of the country. Any product produced anywhere in the country can easily come to the hands of the buyers from any location due to retailing. After Globalization retail business occupies a lion's share in marketing. Now it divert the attention of not only the Govt. but also for research scholars, planers, manufacturers, economists and others in the present scenario.

David Gilbert

The author is one of the noted authorities who in his book titled "Retail Marketing Management" has identified the reasons of growth of Modern Retailing. In this book he has tried to find out why the growth of retailing is actually taking place. According to him more than any other business we are witnessing the emergence of new forms of retailing and becoming more segmented with reforms focusing on the needs of particular consumer segment. The result of this is the development of more consumer friendly environment. Whereas, once it was manufacturers brand that were all important. The year 2000 has witnessed the power of retailers brand challenging the position of suppliers. The traditional forms of independently owned small business and co-operative have lost significant market share in developed economy and the retail sector is now characterized by large scale, multiple store, run by powerful & sophisticated organizations. The increasing size of retailers and intensifying rates of competition in the markets in which they are operating has made retailers to search for new ways to grow their business. The author has tried to emphasize on two facts: First, retailing has become a major avenue of growth & the increase in the retail operations has changed the market dimensions. Second thing, there is an impact of E-retailing which attracts considerable attention. However, though initially it may not be successful but in the due course of time successful models for retail sectors based on E-business and Electronic Media will definitely influence the multichannel retailing system.

Andrew Newmen & Peter Cullen

The authors in their book 'Retailing: Environment & Operations' have rightly concentrated on understanding various aspects of Retailing as a Business. They have considered retailing as a vibrant part of our changing society and major source of employment. They have noticed that retailing is closely tied to the changing moods of the consumers and new ways of business, spread on by the impressive development in Technology and Management Theory. The book provides a comprehensive grounding in many facets of retailing, including Logistics and Distribution, Merchandising, Store Layout and design, pricing and location strategy. The authors have included new areas of importance which includes retail services and out of store retailing. The authors have tried to understand what are the ways and means because of which retailing is growing in a global scenario? How it has influenced non-formal ways of trading? And what are the implications of new format of retailing on consumer behaviour? In this book the authors have also tried to find out the different market structures that are required for retail operations and managing in the times of booms and slumps. This helps the readers to understand different facets, challenges and changes that are happening in the retail environment.

Michael Levy & Barton Weitz

The authors in their book 'Retailing Management' have tried to know how retailing has become an important economic activity. The book titled 'Retailing Management' is definitely a different form of commentary on 'Retailing Operations' especially in the modern & the Western World. The book discusses different facets of retailing strategies as they are useful for developing the retail markets especially in a growing economy. In this book the authors have tried to find out the reasons of growth of modern retailing, different retail format, and multichannel retailing as a method of operating in a competitive market. From the author's point of view there is a great change in the consumer behaviour which is influencing the pattern of retailing and their strategies. The consumers have changed not only in terms of perception, choices & ideas and identities but also their modes of buying have significantly varied. These changes in the formats of retailing cannot convince the consumers as to why they should buy the particular product from a particular retail outlet. The change in the formats of branding i.e. from manufacturing brand to retail branding or private labelling has also proved to be of a limited impact. Therefore new methods of promotion especially attracting and retaining consumer, changes in the POP display system are being introduced. The buying system has changed, so does the buying methods and promotional methods also have changed. The retailers have tried to introduce new pricing strategy and the retail communication has become a more important aspect of retail management in the modern world.

Barry Burman and Joel Evans

The authors have offered a different kind of approach to the present system of retailing. The book 'Retail Management: A Strategic Approach' is basically related with understanding the marketing phenomenon of retailing, the changes brought in due to competition amongst retailers in terms of marketing, distribution, as well as promotional practices. The author has concentrated on understanding and analyzing the detailed market from different dimensions. The concept of SWOT analysis, situation analysis and tactical analysis has been adopted by the authors to understand new trends in retail marketing, its implications on competition as well as economics of retailing, changes in the pricing policy and promotional techniques that are adopted by different organized large scale retailers. The authors have tried to understand retail institutions in terms of ownership, in terms of demand pattern, in terms of strategic mix, in terms of emerging forms. The authors have noticed that the non-traditional retailing especially Web Stores, or Electronic Retail Channels are becoming more profitable and popular because of changing tastes and styles of buyers, because of liking of the new and emerging trend of Electronic medium. Internet has influenced not only in terms of technology but Internet has become a social medium of communication, which is responsible for development of E-Retailing which has drastically influenced the strategies of retail management. This has changed the perception, competitive strategies, distribution systems and promotional strategies that are adopted by the retailers.

3 Review Of Ph.D. Thesis

Kittima Cheungsuvadee (2006)

The author in her thesis titled "Business adaptation strategies used by small and Medium retailers in an increasingly competitive Environment: a study of Ubon Ratchathani, Thailand Studied business adaptation strategies employed by small and Medium retailers in order to be sustainable in a climate of rapid and significant Environmental change in regional thailand. The study was carried out in ubon Ratchathani, a large regional city in north eastern thailand which shares many of the difficulties encountered by regional businesses in regional thailand. Changes Over the last ten years have been considered in this work and recent strategies adopted by the small and medium retailers have been investigated. The study shows there are major deficiencies in the capabilities of many of the small Businesses and that these need to be addressed by government. Smaller businesses do not have the same access to the resources of larger businesses and chain stores but can become more competitive through effective use of networks or business Associations which the government needs to support. The author proposes that an Existing government initiative to promote one tambon one product could be Expanded to provide resources and networks which could be utilised by small businesses to become more sustainable and make a greater contribution to the Economy. The findings of this study also show that the main lack of capability is in the Accounting and management area in the smaller businesses and the author advocates Provision of an extensive training program through regional educational institutions.

Richard John Speed (1991)

The author in his thesis titled "Marketing, strategy and performance in the UK retail financial services industry" seeks to examine the marketing practices, strategies and organisational characteristics of companies in the UK retail financial services industry. The research utilises both quantitative and qualitative methods, seeking to determine what, if any, differences in approach exist between companies of different types or with different levels of performance. Three methods are used to evaluate performance; self assessment, peer assessment and expert assessment. Data was gathered using a semi-structured questionnaire as the basis for interviews with managers.

Quantitative analysis utilised contingency table analysis and discriminant analysis to test for differences between different groups of companies. Account was taken of problems due to small sample size. The Delphi technique, a form of anonymous polling of experts over several rounds with feedback between rounds, was used to construct the expert assessment based measure of performance. Companies with better performance were found to have a different strategy from those with poor performance. Better performing companies were found to have products better at meeting customer needs than those of competitors, and to charge more for them. Better performing companies were found to be faster at new product development and to show a balance in their strategy between finance and market performance based factors. Companies of different types were also found to differ in their marketing approaches. A high level of consistency was found between the various measures of performance used. The measures were highly correlated and the sets of variables found to be related to performance level measured by different means had considerable overlap.

4 Review Of Research Papers

Prof. Prem Vrat (2010)

The authors in this paper focuses primarily on the Small and Medium Scale Retail Sector of India which is largely unorganized. Faced by stiff competition from major enterprises like Reliance and Wal-Mart, that allocate considerable amount of resources on research and development of tools for increasing competitiveness and efficiency, a systematic study on the application of Industrial Engineering Principles in unorganized retail sector is an important area of study and of relevance to the Indian Economy. The paper attempts to present an in-depth study of retail sector of India, organized and unorganized, and identifies parameters for defining competitiveness in the context of Indian Retail. Integrating Quality Function Deployment (QFD) analysis with the Kano model the paper highlights major technical issues related to Kirana and Apparel Shops. A model for optimizing product assortment in a small unorganized store has been presented, with the introduction of the concept of linear cross elasticity. It highlights the managerial insights gained through the study.

Aluregowda (2013)

The author through his study opined that the Indian retail has traditionally been an unorganized sector, where retailers lacked the means as well as the will to develop or expand. Retail could also never enjoy the support of the Indian consumer, who is famous for being miserly and who treats shopping as a form of leisure, enjoying the thrill of discovering bargains and discount deals in his own time. The western attitude of splurging, indulging and shop-till-you drop has slowly entered the country and led to organized retailing. The purpose of the study is to determine the influence of selected strategies on the growth of the business. The convenience sampling method was used and the data was collected from the loyal world supermarket managers. The results revealed that all the selected strategies are positively related to growth of the business

Walsh, Gianfranco and Hennig – Thurau (2001)

The authors in their study observed that there is a lack of previous relevant consumer research in Germany, together with the need to test the generalizability of consumer decision making styles in different countries and with non – student samples prompted an investigation of German shoppers. The original U.S. eight factor model could not be confirmed completely, but support was found for six factors: Brand Consciousness, Perfectionism, Recreational/Hedonism and Confused by over choice, Impulsiveness and Novelty – Fashion Consciousness. Variety seeking was novel to Germany and replaced brand loyalty and price value consciousness factors found in previous countries.

Trail, Bruce (2006)

The author conducted study about analysed the rapid spread of supermarkets in developing and middle income countries and forecast its continuation. In this article, the level of supermarket penetration is modelled quantitatively on a cross section of 42 countries for which data could be obtained, representing all stages of development. This study has found that: GDP per capita income distribution, urbanization. Female labour force participation and openness to inward foreign investment are all significant explicators.

Bhat and Bowonder (2001)

The author analysed the experience of interweaving brand reputation organizational and technological innovation. The authors observed that the effective management of innovation involves creatively managing process of creative destruction. For a product like a watch, capturing market share requires the careful enmeshing of brand reputation and innovation. Positioning itself uniquely through a comprehensive visioning exercise, Titan became a market leader. Titan industries became the most admired brand in selling watches in forty countries.

Welsh and Falbe (2006)

The researchers conducted a research on international retail franchising. The study begins with an overview of the development of the literature and then discusses the nature and scope of emerging markets, with particular reference to their impact on the stakeholders of international retail franchising. Then the article develops a conceptual model retailing international retail franchising to its stakeholders.

Shim et. Al (2001)

The authors through their indicate that an attitude toward a behaviour can be recognized by an individual's positive or formats negative evaluation of a relevant behaviour which comprises a person's beliefs regarding the perceived outcomes of performing the behaviour. From this perspective knowledge of consumer's attitudes can help explain the reasons behind their favourable and unfavourable evaluations of an object or behaviour for example why consumers do or do not buy products of particular brand names or shop at certain types of store.

Magleburg et al. (2004)

The author through their research opined that the teenagers who shop often with their friends are more vulnerable to informational influence and less prone to normative influence.

Prus (1993)

The author in a qualitative study said that a number of dilemmas for consumers are created by shopping companions like additional definitions (encouragements, discouragements and distractions) of products, money, users as well as their concerns with the identities and ensuing relationships implied by the presence of their companions.

Mascarenhas and Higby (1993)

The authors discovered the interpersonal influences in teenagers and found three major influence sources were considered peers, parents and the media. The above studies do not specifically focus on apparel retail sector in Indian context. Moreover, the above studies focus more on factors influencing store choice behaviour as well as shopping behaviour and do not identify the profile of customers who are visiting this new-generation retail outlets which is very important for the marketer to attract customers inside the store. Also it is very important to know as the retail stores in organized sector are growing day by day in numbers whether customers are actually satisfied with the retail outlets. However, this study specifically focuses on apparel retail sector in the Indian context to identify profile of retail customers and measure their level of satisfaction with the present day retail outlets.

Rees (1992)

The author in his study revealed that factors influencing the consumer's choice of food are complex and must be added to variables such as flavor, texture, appearance, advertising etc. Demographic and household role changes and the introduction of microwave ovens have produced changes in eating habits, a reduction in traditional cooking, fragmentation of family means and an increase in 'snacking'. The vigorous sale of chilled and other prepared foods is related to the large numbers of working wives and single people, who require and value convenience. Developments in retailing with concentration of 80per cent of food sales in supermarkets, is also important. Consumers are responding to messages about safety and healthy eating they are concerned about the way in which food is produced and want safe, 'natural', high quality food at an appropriate price.

Ragavan (1994)

The author reported that quality, regular availability, price, accuracy in weighing and billing, range of vegetables and accessibility as the factors in the order of importance which had influenced purchase of vegetables by respondents from modern retail outlets.

Hugar and Vijay Kumar (1996)

The authors carried out a study in Dharwad city to identify various factors that influence the consumption of vegetables. A sample of 90 consumers was chosen at random. It was observed that the personal attributes such as educational level and sex had significant influence on the quantity and frequency of purchase. Price had a high influence on quantity purchased among the lower income group but the effect was not pronounced for high income groups.

Sundar (1997)

The study revealed that the Grocery Department of Saravana Bava cooperative supermarket, Cuddalore was enjoying favorable images of consumers in the attributes such as equality of price, behavior of sales persons, moving space, location, correctness of weight, packaging of goods, number of sales persons and convenient shopping hours. At the same time, the image is weak in the attributes such as quality of goods, availability of range of products, variety of goods, acceptance of returns, credit facility, and door delivery and in sales promotional measures.

Chung et al. (1998)

The authors through their study revealed the factors influencing the furniture retailer purchasing decisions in Taiwan. Important factors of the furniture producers in choosing distribution channel were production capacity, salesmanship, type and grade of the products, transportation and storage. Many distribution channels were available to the producers. The retailers were under pressure to reconsider their management style and marketing strategy in order to obtain more profit. The most important business concerns to the retailers were the product quality and the number of locations selling the same furniture. The salesman in the furniture business agreed that education and training were very important, with 96.70 per cent of the retailers believing that service mentality was the most important requirement for salesman. The factors influencing the retailer's decision to purchase furniture were product
Quality (100%), Style of finishing (100%), special functions (90%), assembly functions (90%), cheap price (90%) and the reputation of suppliers (90%).

Sanjaya *et al* (2000)

The authors in their study on buying behavior for branded fine rice in Chennai and Coimbatore city observed that the quality and image of the brand were important factor for proffering it and also noted that price was not the most important factor for the affluent people in both cities.

Burke (2001)

The author has created a brand equity index comprised of three components, best described as brand equity molecule, which is overarching device of brand equity molecule, which is overarching device of retaining and attracting customers. The three atoms which embedded to molecule were (i) image, (ii) value and (iii) loyalty. Image and value perceptions pull in new customers while loyalty and value retain customer.

Sharma and Jaglekar (2001)

The authors surveyed 4000 households in the area of Godavari – Co- operative dairy (GCD) in Rajahmundry, Andhra Pradesh. One of the main purpose of this survey was to ascertain the attitudes of consumers towards quality of dairy milk. The results revealed that more than 59 per cent of the families expressed that the milk supplied by the GDC was of medium quality. About 32 per cent of the families consider that the milk was primarily judged on the basis of level of content.

Nandagopal and Chinnaiyan (2002)

The researchers conducted a study on brand preference of soft drinks in rural Tamil Nadu using Garrets ranking techniques to rank factors influencing the soft drinks preferred by rural consumers. They found that the product quality was ranked as first followed by retail price. Good quality was ranked as first followed by retail price. Good quality and availability were the main factors which influence the rural consumers of a particular brand of a product.

Devlin *et al.* (2003)

The authors conducted a study on means-end chain analysis of the food sector and explored the extent to which the findings made can be used to inform the retail positioning strategy of food retailers in the UK, using data obtained from 15 respondents. Using means-end theory as the theoretical underpinning of the study, the study employed laddering methodology to identify the linkages between food retail store attributes and personal values. The findings of the study presented a more personally relevant representation of consumer's perceptual orientations towards food retail store image. At the attribute level "good quality products", "good reputation", "store has additional services", and "value for money", are most sought after. These were linked to the consequences "feel good" and to "save time". Overall, the findings support previous value driven research, concluding that "happiness" and "quality of life" were the most strived for personal values.

Cavard and Moreau (2003)

The authors undertook a survey among 2000 French consumers in 2002 to study their behavior regarding the purchase of fruit and vegetables. It first appraised purchasing frequency; the weekly purchase being prevalent. Regarding places of purchase, supermarkets come first, followed closely by markets. In terms of modes of purchase, the self service with assisted weighing was the preferred option. Consumer expectations concern better control of labeling and quality on the selling place, with an indication of consumed-by date. The main consumers, the old-aged people, appear, however, to be less concerned with this additional information.

Michels *et al.* (2003)

The study revealed that almost all food retailers in Germany sold organic products, fresh ones being estimated at 45per cent of the turnover. Surveys indicated that 49.7 per cent of households bought fresh products, principally vegetables, at least once between April and December 2002.

Vegetables, fruit, potatoes, and eggs were the main categories on offer in supermarket-type outlets; specialist whole food shops and producers' direct marketing enterprises carried a wider range of produce including meat. Some 77 per cent of turnover by the larger retailers was from sales to regular purchasers. Average frequency of purchasing, however, was not over Fie times in Nine months. Younger customers tended to buy from specialist outlets rather than supermarkets.

Manivannan and Raghunanthan (2004)

The authors observed that there was no close relationship between the age, sex, education, occupation and extend of utilizing departmental stores where as income alone had shown a close relationship with the extent of utilizing departmental store at 1per cent significant level, which shows that there was a close relationship between income and extent of utilizing department stores.

Kinsey *et al.* (2004)

The authors in his study identified seven forces that had converged to create a demand-driven food system in the USA were (1) more diverse consumer characteristics and tastes; (2) the universal product code (bar code) and all the information technology that followed; (3) Wal-Mart (biggest food retailer in the world), the early adopter of information technology and the mother of efficient supply chain management; (4) efficient consumer response, a defensive response to Wal-Mart's expansion; (5) Concentration of retail ownerships; (6) global concentration of food processing and manufacturing; and (7) new business models.

Sezen (2004)

The author conducted a study on the pricing strategy for perishable products, found that consumers were less likely to purchase perishable goods when their expiry dates are near. For this reason, retailers frequently implement a discount pricing policy when the products have reached closer to their expiry dates. Thus the retailers tend to gain by reducing losses due to spoilage of goods.

McLaughten (2004)

The author in the study of the dynamics of fresh fruits and vegetable pricing in the super market channel, he concluded that major factor that contribute to the complicated price formation process, of several levels, of fruit and vegetables in the US were marketing channels, market structure changes, pricing techniques and promotional impacts, retail responses to supply changes, and price versus value.

Haese *et al.* (2005)

The study revealed that since late 1990s, the number of supermarkets in South Africa has been steadily growing. Due to a more effective and efficient management and procurement system, the supermarkets can benefit from economies of scale and sell food at a relative low price. In their study they presented a case study of two villages in the Transkei area of South Africa. In these poor rural communities, the majority of households now buy their main food items from supermarkets rather than from local shops and farmers. While presenting an important step towards livelihood development and food security, these supermarkets also form a strong competitor for local agricultural sales. The supermarkets provide many food items at lower prices. With an increase in income, the households look for variety and exoticism in their food products, and will most likely find this in the supermarkets, rather than the local stores.

Li Lan *et al.* (2006)

The author conducted a study on Food retailers pricing and marketing strategies and found out that retail grocery chains were the dominant players in the vertical market channels for many commodities. Retailers through mechanism of vertical control exert a strong influence on upstream suppliers and determine the products offered in their stores. They also noted that large retailers posses some degree of oligopoly. The small scale producers' revenue decreases when retailers use promotional sales as a selling strategy although the consumers were benefited.

Rajesh Shinde (2007)

The author in his study on recent facets of consumer behavior in two villages of Aurangabad District of Maharashtra state observed that in the village Balanagar, 14 respondents (28%) reported that price factor was taken into account, 10 respondents (20%) reported that quality factor was more important for them, 8 respondents (16%) reported that availability was considered while purchasing, 18 respondents (36%) reported that small size was preferred while purchasing. In Pimpalwadi village 11respondents (22%) reported that price was an important factor while purchasing, 14 respondents (28%) reported that they prefer quality, 10 respondents (20%) reported that they purchased according to the availability of the product, 15 respondents (30%) reported that they had taken into account small size while purchasing the fast moving consumer goods (FMCG) product.

Halepete *et al.* (2008),

The author's outlines that in times of cut throat competition in the retail industry and saturation of domestic markets; retailers have been looking to expand internationally. Wal-Mart as a company that has been expanding internationally for several years is now entering into the Indian retail market in a partnership with Bharti Enterprises in India. The main objective of this study was to explore the challenges that Wal-Mart might face as it expands into the Indian retail market. Wal-Mart's failures in Germany and South Korea are analyzed to identify the lessons that can be learned from these failures so that these lessons can be put to good use in the Indian market. The results of the study show that the main reason for Wal-Mart's failure in Germany and South Korea are the cultural differences between consumers, lack of understanding of the consumer, high cost of real-estate and aggressive competition etc. This operating model in India has the potential to expose Wall-Mart to potential challenges. Although there is a large population in India, the diversity and heterogeneity of the Indian market is tremendously complex. Diverse religions, languages, value systems, food habits, economic buying power, clothing selection and access to transportation are the attributes that clearly demonstrate the complexity in India. The biggest challenge for Wal-Mart in India is the competition from organized and unorganized sector, different customers' mindsets, value-conscious shoppers etc. This significant challenge needs to be well-understood and suitably addressed for success in the Indian market.

Jasola (2007)

The study by the author explores the emerging trends in new retailing formats and strategic issues of retailers. The author is of the view that India's vast middle class and untapped retail industry are the key attraction for global retail giants wanting to enter new markets. Malls, speciality stores, discount stores, department stores, hypermarkets, supermarkets, convenience stores and multi-brand outlets are most preferred retail formats in India. Malls lend an ideal shopping experience with an amalgamation of product, service and entertainment all under one roof. Discount stores offer discount on the MRP through selling in bulk reaching economies of scale. Department stores cater to a variety of consumer needs. Super-markets contribute to 30% of all food and grocery organized retail sales. Convenience stores stock convenience products and prices are slightly higher due to the convenience premium. The study further points out that the share of modern retail is likely to grow from its current 2% to 15-20% over the next decade.

Gupta (2007)

The study by the author reveals that the retail sector of a country reflects its socio-demographic characteristics. The size and density of retail outlets are influenced by demand related phenomena such as population density, level of urbanization, participation rate of women in the labour force, access to cars, taste and personal consumption expenditure. With the changing socio-economic scenario in India, the dynamics of retail have also undergone a sea change. Product, place, price, promotion, people and process play an important role in retailing. On the other hand, physical evidence is one aspect that does not need any emphasis at all due to changing mindset of consumers.

Bhardwaj and Makkar (2007)

The authors opine that NCR and Mumbai will continue to dominate the Indian retail scene and despite strong growth in secondary and tertiary cities, these metros will still account for 40% of India's organized retail sector by 2008. Both are large and diverse to accommodate a variety of new formats, including one-stop malls, speciality malls, hyper markets and big-box retailing. The researcher is of the view that secondary metros are perceived by retailers as the "next retail destinations" which throw a strong challenge to Mumbai and NCR Region. Pune, Bangalore, Kolkata, Hyderabad and Ahmadabad all have significant mall.

Shukla (2007)

The author is of the view that the world is now looking at India as the nation of the future. More significantly, India is well on its way to emerging as a first-world economy in the fields of information technology, biotechnology, pharmaceuticals, food and grocery and automotive sectors. Food and groceries, health and beauty, apparel, jewellery and consumer durables are the fastest growing categories of organized retail. Currently, the fashion sector in India commands a lion's share in the organized retail pie. Retail trade takes place in India through different types of outlets - kirana shops, modern retail shops, discount stores, departmental stores, supermarkets and hypermarkets. Kirana shops are features of our landscape which store goods unpackaged in bulk containers. In 2002-2003, Indians in some cities got the taste of discount stores for the first time. The discount stores emerged as "class-less stores" with consumers of all income levels shopping at these stores. Favourable demographic and psychographic changes relating to India's consumer class, international exposure, availability of products and brands communication are some of the factors that are driving the retail in India. Franchising is emerging as the preferred option for global retailers. The study suggests India will have to arrive at its unique formats of retailing in order to tap the market and this requires significant capital, technology and the best practices to bridge the existing productivity gaps, which are critical to the sector's success.

Mishra (2008)

The study depicts that the economic growth, demographics, increasing income, purchasing power and changing Indian consumers are the various factors behind growth of organized retail market which leads to a large number of retailers, necessitates better enforcement of taxation and introduction of an efficient labor law monitoring system. Organized retailing in most economies has typically passed through four distinct phases in its evolution cycle - new retail entrant driving growth, consumer demand organized formats, retailer strengthening backend system and retailers going global. India is currently in the second phase of evolution, i.e., consumer demand organized formats. The study further reveals that mall space, demography, rising young population, availability of brands, rising retail finance, changing.

Satish and Raju (2010)

A recent study by the authors points out that the retail sector is at an inflexion point where the growth of organized retailing and growth in the consumption by the Indian population will take a higher growth trajectory. The Indian retail industry has strong linkages with the economic growth and development of the economy. The study throws light on the major Indian retailers which contribute highly to the retail sector in India.

Erdem *et al.* (1999)

The author examines the linkages between consumer values and the importance of some salient store attributes. The findings of the exploratory study indicated that the important judgments for store attributes were influenced by the set of terminal and instrumental values viewed as important by the shoppers. Even though the importance of store attributes was related to both kinds of values, it seems that there was a disproportionate predominance of terminal values in this influence. In addition, combining values with demographic information can provide a better understanding of targeted consumers, and marketing programs based on this understanding can enhance the effectiveness of retail management.

Gupta (2004)

The author stated that in the Indian economy, branding has emerged as an important marketing tool and brands play an important role in facing competition. Ranging from the shopkeeper to the most sophisticated supermarkets, departmental stores, plazas and malls which provide the latest and better quality products, the customer now has multiple options to choose from. The study tries to explore the purchase behaviour of consumers with respect to items of daily needs and the type of shops they patronized. The survey was conducted in the city of Ghaziabad and proportionate stratified sampling was used. The results of the study show that people generally prefer to purchase and stock for a month rather than keep purchasing frequently. Although different categories of products are purchased from the different types of shops, department stores and wholesale shops emerge as consumers' first choice.

Morschett *et al.* (2005),

According to shopping motives influence the perception of retail store attributes as well as the attitude towards retail stores. An empirical study was carried out in Germany with 560 grocery shoppers using quota sampling method. The study highlights that on the basis of four central dimensions of shopping motives (scope orientation, quality orientation, price orientation and time orientation), a taxonomic analysis has been done which identified the four segments of shoppers differing significantly in the configuration of motives expecting to be satisfied by the shopping activity: (1) one-stop shoppers, (2) time-pressed price shoppers, (3) dedicated quality shoppers, and (4) demanding shoppers. Finally the results support the proposition that consumers differ in their attitude towards a grocery store according to their shopping motives.

Jackson *et al.* (2006)

The study by aims to understand how the changing forms of retail provision are experienced at the neighbourhood and household level in the Portsmouth area of England. The study demonstrates that consumer choice between stores can be understood in terms of accessibility and convenience, whereas choice within stores involves notions of value, price, and quality. The choice between and within stores is strongly mediated by consumers' household contexts, reflecting the extent to which shopping practices are embedded within consumers' domestic routines and complexities in everyday lives.

Srivastava (2008)

According to the increase in the number of retail chains across the country is an indication that organized retailing is emerging as an industry and will boom in a big way in the near future. The sector has more than 12 million retail outlets. It has the highest retail destiny in the world and in terms of ownership, it primarily consists of independent, owner managed shops. The emerging modern large scale formats viz. supermarkets, speciality stores, chain stores, department stores, hypermarkets, factory outlets and discount stores have transformed the retailing environment in India. Malls comprise of 90% of the total future retail development. A significant trend in the market is the development of a combination of retail and entertainment centres. Malls with multiplexes such as cinema theatres, food courts and play places for children are becoming the centres for family outings. Household groceries, food and apparel are the key drivers in Indian retail industry.

Rajagopal (2009)

The study examines the impact of growing congestion of shopping malls in urban areas on shopping convenience and shopping behaviour. This study referred to personality traits of shoppers affecting the preferences for shopping malls in reference to store assortment, convenience, and economic advantage and leisure facilities. The study was held on urban areas of Mexico during 2005-2008 during different festival seasons mainly April - June (spring sales, Mother's day and Father's day), July - August (summer sales) and November - January (winter sales and Christmas celebrations). Five point likert scale, structural equation model and regression techniques have been used for analysis. The results of the study show that narrowing the shopping streets and the rise of shopping malls has been major trends in retailing in emerging markets. The ambience of shopping malls, assortment of stores, sales promotions and comparative economic gains are the major factors which attract higher customer traffic to the mall.

5 Concluding Remarks

This Chapter gives a brief summary of the literature review of the studies favouring overall retail scenario, consumers' perspective including attributes of retailing and consumer preferences and choice of store and retailers' perspective covering the studies related to marketing strategies of retailers'. Based on the review, the study underlines the existing gaps and presents a theoretical framework for undertaking research in this area.

CHAPTER III
THEORETICAL CONCEPT OF MARKETING

1. Introduction

In this chapter the marketing concepts and models will be explained, that will conceptualise the problem statement and objectives of the study. In addition this chapter will give an in-depth understanding of the marketing concepts and models that relate to the study, as well as define important elements that will give the reader a better understanding of the background of the study.

2. Marketing

Kotler and Armstrong (2008), interpret marketing as "a social and managerial process by which individuals and groups obtain what they need and want through creating and exchanging products and value with others." Although there are several definitions of the main function of marketing, the core message is that of attracting consumers.

Attracting consumers can be achieved through satisfying consumer's needs and wants. Although the message is simple, this process can be complex as consumer-buying patterns are changing, while consumers are also becoming more knowledgeable about product offerings, resulting in them becoming more analytical. Consequently, consumers are willing to pay more for a product, which they perceive to be of good quality. Organisations are presently faced with a challenge of gathering knowledge and understanding their consumers and offering them products that exceed their expectations (Kotler & Armstrong, 2008:5).

Marketing aims to create and satisfy consumers' needs and wants. This can be achieved through developing an efficient marketing strategy that attracts new consumers and creates an advantage over competitors. The diagram below illustrates the main idea of marketing.

Figure 3.1 is a Model Of Marketing

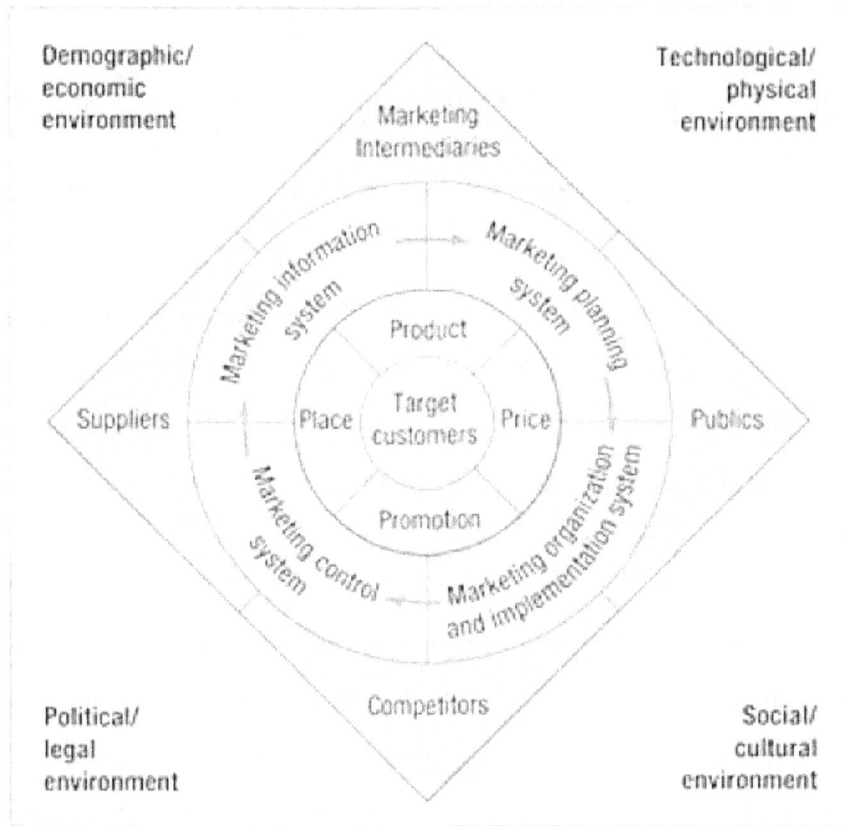

Figure 3.1 is a Model of marketing, which shows the different stages used when creating a marketing strategy. The first stage is to know how each organisation perceives marketing, and what they would like to achieve with the marketing strategy. A marketing audit can be used to analyse the position and opportunity that an organisation has in the market place, through market analysis, marketing segmentations and marketing strategy.

Marketing research is used to gain information on the market as shown in Figure 3.1 and this can be done using quantitative analysis, qualitative analysis or consumer tests. The last stage is to make use of the marketing mix tools, which will be used to persuade consumers to purchase certain products and services. The marketing mix is made up of four elements namely, product, price, place and promotion (Kotler & Armstrong, 2008:27).

3. The Marketing Mix

According to Kotler (2003:127), in order to create a successful marketing strategy, the marketing mix must reflect desires of the consumers in the target market. The marketing mix comprises of product, price, promotion and place. These controllable variables can be altered and adjusted to suit the organisation's objectives. It is, therefore, vital for organisations to make use of this strategic planning process, and to match the needs of the consumer with the organisation's marketing strategy (Kotler, 2003:128).

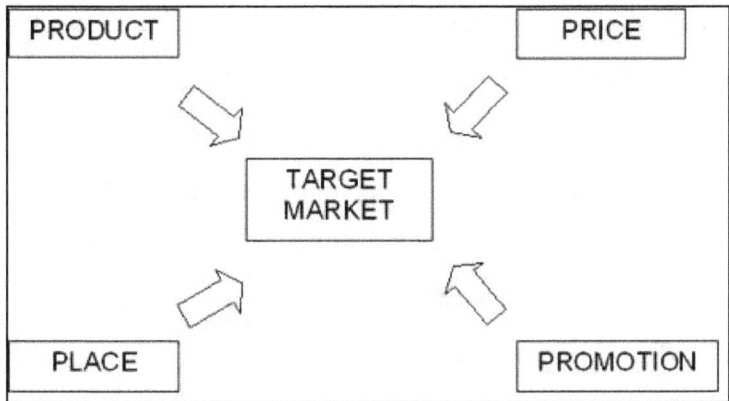

Figure 3.2: Marketing Mix Tools

(Kotler, 2003:26)

Figure 2.6 is a model of the marketing mix tools. The marketing mix tools are a set of tools, which organisations use to realise their marketing strategies. The marketing mix, which is also called the 4P's, and how it has adapted during the economic downturn highlights the basis of this study. The elements of the marketing mix are controllable variables, which should be managed in the correct way in order to meet the needs of the defined target group (Kotler, 2003:25).

Table 3.1: Characteristics of the Marketing Mix

(Kotler, 2003:23)

Product	Price	Promotion	Place
Functionality	List price	Advertising	Where you sell your product
Appearance	Discounts	Personal selling	Physical boundaries defining the business
Quality	Financing	Public relations	Retail space
Packaging	What you have in stock versus sold	Message	The service
Brand	Reflect brand image	Media	Product (shipped, purchased from the company etc.)
Warranty	Period in months or years	Budget	Store

The function of the marketing mix variables is to maximise the performance of the organisation by combining different variables to satisfy the needs of consumers. The challenge, however, is that organisations are under pressure to adjust their marketing strategies to suit new market demands, which are caused by changes of consumer buying behaviour. The marketing mix elements comprise of products, price, place and promotions. These are discussed below.

Product mix

Products can be divided into two sections, namely consumer products, which are for personal use or enjoyment, and business products, which are bought for resale or use in a business (Ferrell & Hartline, 2007:60). The use of the word product can also be used to describe a service offered by an organisation. Moreover, business products or, as Kotler and Armstrong (2008:42) define them, industrial products are often characterised by derived demand. Organisations are building better relationships with their suppliers in order to meet consumer's demands as well as satisfy economies of scale (Kotler & Armstrong, 2008:42). Most organisations do not sell only one product, but one or several product lines. By doing this, they can spread the risks among different product lines (Ferrell & Hartline, 2007:50).According to Kotler (2003:22), "while organisations are selling a product, consumers are buying a solution." The way organisations offer these solutions should be thought of with careful consideration of competitive forces. As more products are placed on the market, and offer solutions to consumers, organisations are finding it more difficult to come up with innovative solutions. This is a result of consumers becoming more knowledgeable about product offerings and benefits. These products can be perceived in various ways, which include physical make-up, as well as the availability and branding of products. The product can be offered in the following ways: (1) core product, which is the core benefit that the consumer can profit from; (2) actual product is what the consumers perceive the brand to be over competitor products, which is done through branding, added benefits, extra features and so on; and (3) augmented products are the added non-tangible offering that an organisation can use, for example, additional services, delivery and so forth. Organisations are now offering more than one product line in order to reduce the risk by spreading it amongst different products (Porter, 1998:364).

Branding

Branding is the process through which a product is given a name, logo and design. Organisations use branding to create a perception about the product and to set it apart from their competition. Consumers now have the task of choosing the brand of product that they would like to buy, and there are several factors that affect this decision process. Branding is supposed to add value to the product by creating a relationship with the target market (Randall, 2000:3). Organisations that have mastered the art of branding have reaped the benefits of creating a bond with consumers, as more and more consumers have become loyal to specific brands. The power that organisations now have through branding is that consumers instantaneously buy a brand of a product even if there is a substitute product that offers a cheaper price. Such brands have loyal consumers that have confidence and believe in what the brand represents. Consequently, these organisations have a solid foundation that makes it difficult for new entrants to compete with this brand (Randall, 2000:4).

Packaging

Packaging is how the product is presented on the exterior. The use of packaging has transformed to more than mere product packaging. It ranges from organisation brochures, organisation uniforms, their offices and all the other visuals of the organisation. Packaging is even regarded as the fifth marketing element after product, price, promotion and place. The importance of packaging as a tool in marketing has spread to other functions because of the increased competition from other products. Packaging has the function of attracting consumer attention, informing consumers of the product and, finally, making the sale. Rising consumer wealth has led consumers to spend more on products that offer more than merely the solution; consumers strive for packaging that offers confidence and prestige (Ferrell & Hartline, 2007:201).

Price mix

Price differs from the other three elements, since it is the only marketing element that generates direct turnover. Marketers should seek to find the optimum balance between cutting costs and making maximum profits, without negatively influencing the volume of production (Kotler, 1999:33). The price should reflect the supply and demand relationship (Kotler & Armstrong, 1996:40). Price is the only element in the marketing mix that creates direct revenue. When planning the price of a product there are several pricing strategies, which should be considered. These are: (1) penetration pricing; (2) skimming pricing; (3) competition pricing; (4) product line pricing; (5) bundle pricing; (6) psychological pricing; (7) premium pricing; and (8) optional pricing. These strategies are dependent on objectives that the organisation wants to achieve (Kotler & Armstrong, 2008:279). Furthermore, pricing is the marketing variable that is the easiest to change (Ferrell & Hartline, 2007:55). While the product or promotion can take months to change, the price can be changed directly. Except from being the easiest and fastest to change, pricing is also the cheapest to change. While changing promotion, products or distribution is usually quite costly; the opposite is true when it involves the price element. The price is an important factor that consumers consider, especially during economical downturns. During these times organisations are forced to make radical changes in their price decisions (Shama, 2006:43). The most common decision is to increase sales volume through price cuts. Conversely, this could lead to problems in the long term by lowered profitability. Organisations should ensure that the price changing is in line with their organisational objectives and that they do not send mixed signals about the product (Kotler & Armstrong, 2007:279).

During an economic downturn consumers change their buying patterns by being more cautious about what they buy. Price becomes an important factor for consumers at this stage. Organisations should ensure that the changes that are made to the marketing mix elements are in line with the needs of the target market, and that the market environment is suitable for all changes that are made. (Business Review Weekly, 2000).

Kotler (2003:28) argues that *"pricing is an important but difficult issue in the marketing mix model; important because it is the only element that generates turnover for the organisation, while all the other elements are connected to costs and pricing, which are difficult because the various products have demand and cost interrelationship and are subject to different degrees of competition."*

Pricing strategies

Kotler (2003:59) reduces the various strategies to three primary strategies that are involved when pricing any product:

    Skimming   : Make money by charging higher prices.
    Penetration   : Price lower and gain market share.

Neutral   : Be competitive with competition.

The three primary strategies are discussed further in this section. When setting prices, an organisation can adopt a number of pricing strategies, which are based on objectives that the organisation wants to achieve, for example, penetration pricing; low prices to increase sales, skimming pricing; high price in the beginning and then slow lowering to reach a wider market, and competition pricing; and price in comparison with competitors (Kotler, & Armstrong, 2002:35). The three primary strategies are discussed below:

1) **Skimming pricing**

The objective here is to skim profits off the market. The organisation sets an initial high price and then slowly lowers the price to make the product available to a wider market. It is usually used in high-technological markets. It is a main strategy when a new product is launched. Firstly, the product is dedicated to innovators, while prices are then slowly decreased so that products become available for early adopters.

2) **Penetration pricing**

An organisation sets low prices in order to increase sales and market share. It is an effective strategy when an organisation wants to gain a market share, however it can be risky. Competitors can also low their prices instead not to lose market share. Hence, not only can an organisation gain market share, but it can also lose part of the profits.

3) **Neutral pricing**

The organisation sets a price, which is similar to a competitor's price. It is an effective strategy when the organisation does not want to undersell. Consumers choose a product by comparing the value and price. If the price is at the same level as the substitute product, then the most important factor is value of product (Kotler & Armstrong, 2008:390). Table 2.4 shows the differences between the three strategies: Skimming, penetration and neutral.

Table 3.4: External influences on pricing strategies (Kotler & Armstrong, 2008:390)

	SKIMMING	PENETRATION	NEUTRAL

COSTS	Low cost margin Low volumes Changes in unit price drive profit Large break even sales Changes at or near capacity	High cost margins High volumes Changes in volume drive profitability Small break even sales Changes excess capacity	Costs similar to competitors Sufficient cost margin to finance advantage Little excess capacity Incremental capacity is expensive is expensive
CONSUMERS	Low price sensitivity -Reference price effect -Price quality effect -Difficult comparison effect	High price sensitivity - Total expend effect - Large part of end benefit - Little differentiation	Consumers are more sensitive to other elements of the marketing mix
COMPETITION	Limited threat of opportunism Limited opportunity for scale economies Sustainable differentiation Low threat brands	Sustainable cost and resource advantage Competitors not willing to retaliate Financial strength Aggressive small share brands	Avoid threat of retaliation Large share brands with a lot to lose Sustainable marketing mix advantages Oligopolies

Product mix pricing situations

The product mix pricing situation can be seen in the Table 3.4

Product line pricing

This refers to pricing different products within the same product range at different price points. An example would be a computer manufacturer that offers different computers with different features at different prices. The greater the features and benefits, the more consumers will pay (Doyle & Stern, 2006:54).

1) **Bundle pricing**

The organisation bundles a group of products at a reduced price. It is a type of strategy, which raises the rate of sell. When consumers want to buy products separately, they will pay more than when they buy it in a "bundle".

2) **Psychological pricing**

The seller here will consider the psychology of price and the positioning of price within the market place. For example the seller will, therefore, charge 99 cents instead R1 or R299 instead of R300 (Doyle & Stern, 2006:54).

3) **By Product pricing**

This is pricing a product that will be used in conjunction with the main product. An example of this is zoom lenses that come separate with a camera.

5) **Optional pricing**

The organisation sells optional extras along with the product in order to maximise its turnover. This strategy is commonly used within the car industry. The basic version of the car model can be cheaper than a full version of the same car model (Doyle & Stern, 2006:54).

Placement mix

Place or distribution is the least likely marketing principle to change and the solution to a business's inability to attract consumers. Choice of the right location can be expensive, but larger organisations prefer to employ specialists to find them the best location (Doyle & Stern, 2006:54). Furthermore, the marketing elements include activities such as distribution, transport and store keeping that organisations use to make their products available to consumers ((Kotler, 1999:33). There are several retailers that can be identified, for example, speciality stores, department stores, supermarkets and hypermarkets, which all have different factors, which define them. Unlike smaller retailers, they usually have a narrow but deep assortment and a large focus on high quality service excellence. During the depression of the 1930's in the United States, self-service retailers increased drastically. People were willing to do their "locate-compare selection" on their own in order to save money (Kotler, 1999:33). Non-store retailing can often be a cheaper way to attract consumers. Marketing over the Internet, for example, is a simple and cost effective way to reach out to several consumers at the same time. This communication tool is used by organisations globally, particularly in the retail sector (Kotler, 1999:33).

Distribution

Distribution refers to how the product reaches the consumer, for example, the point of retailing or sale dispersion. The organisation must distribute the product to consumers at the correct place and time. If the organisation wants to achieve its marketing objectives, efficient distribution becomes essential. Profits will be affected if the organisation underestimates demand and consumers cannot purchase products as a result.

Types of distribution

Indirect distribution and direct distribution are two different types of distribution. The difference between the two types of distribution is how the product gets from the organisation to the consumer (Pride & Ferrell, 2010:320).

Distribution strategies

There are three basic distribution strategies, which are available depending on the type of product that is distributed.

§ Intensive distribution

This type of distribution refers to distribution of low priced or impulse products such as soft drinks or sweets. Consumers can buy these products with little effort. Factors that should be determined include time and place. If a consumer cannot locate a product, they will purchase a competitive product (Dowling, 2006:33).

§ Exclusive distribution

This involves narrowing distribution to one organisation. The product is usually in a higher price range and requires more detail in the sale from the mediator, for example, motor vehicles for sale at an exclusive dealer (Dowling, 2006:33).

§ Selective distribution

A small-scale type of retail store is elected to distribute the product. Selective distribution usually occurs with products such as computers, where consumers are more than willing to shop around and where manufacturers want a big geographical spread (Dowling, 2006:33).

Promotion

Products or services that are rendered are successful only if the benefits are clearly communicated to the target market, hence, when organisations decide on their strategy, they should contemplate who their target market is and their behaviour (Kotler & Armstrong, 2008:41). In order to define a target market, an effective message should be created. The message will begin to produce interest from potential consumers, and furthermore make consumers keen to own the product, and in the end make them purchase it. Promotional strategy of an organisation can contain the following: advertising, sales promotion, personal selling and direct mail. Media strategy refers to the way in which an organisation will pitch or deliver their message (Kotler, 1999:32).

Promotion mix

Modern marketing is more than merely producing a good product, availability to targeted consumers and attractive pricing. Organisations should also communicate with their consumers. Promotion mix is an organisation's communication programme, which include a combination of advertising, personal selling, sales promotion and public relations, which the organisation uses to pursue their advertising and marketing objectives (Beamish & Ashford, 2005:103). Marketers have two options when it comes to choosing promotion mix strategies, namely push promotion or pull promotion. The significance of choosing the correct strategy that should be used is critical to the success of the organisation, since the pull and push strategies differ significantly. Hence, marketers should understand both strategies in order to make a correct decision. A push strategy entails 'pushing' the product through distribution channels to the final consumer. Marketers lean towards marketing activities that induce the channel members to promote it to the final consumer (Kotler & Armstrong, 2008:483). By using a pull strategy the marketer guides its marketing activities towards the final buyer, which entices them to buy the product. However, should the pull strategy be effective, consumers will demand the product from channel members who will, therefore, order the demanded product from suppliers. A pull strategy occurs when consumers demand 'pulls' of the product through the channels (Pride & Ferrell, 2010:320). A successful product or service does not mean anything unless the benefits can be clearly communicated to the target market, consequently, when organisations choose their strategy, they should consider their target market and their behaviour (Pride & Ferrell, 2010:320). When the target market is defined, an effective message should be created. This message should attract consumer's attention, arouse their interest, create a desire to own the product and, finally, make them purchase it.

4. Marketing strategies

A marketing strategy demonstrates how an organisation satisfies the needs and wants of consumers. It could also involve other functions that are as important to the business such as maintaining relationships with stakeholders and other business partners. To be more precise, marketing strategy is a plan for how an organisation will use its strengths and capabilities to match the needs and wants of the market (Ferrell & Hartline, 2007:60).

According to Webster (1997), as cited in Hooley, Saunders, Piercy and Nicoulaud (2008:7), "As a strategy, marketing seeks to develop effective responses to changing marketing environments by defining market segments, developing and positioning product offerings for those target markets." Conversely, Johnson and Scholes (2001:105) interpret strategy as "the matching of the activities of an organisation to the environment in which it operates and to its own resources capabilities."

However, even though there are several definitions of a marketing strategy, there is a main understanding that is common amongst all the definitions. A marketing strategy is about doing what is best to meet consumer's expectations, while creating a sense of vision and direction. The development of strategy has two main focus areas, namely general marketing strategies and decision area strategies (Jeannet & Hennessey, 2001:686).

i. General marketing strategies

There are five general marketing strategies and these are: marketing expansion, market share growth, niche market, status quo and market exit strategy.

1) Market expansion

The purpose of market expansion is to increase the number of transactions between organisation and consumers. There are three possible methods for this. The first method aims to increase the frequency with which consumers make purchases from the organisation (for example, by providing benefits for loyal consumers). The second method aims to convince new consumers to make purchases (possibly by making products more attractive through advertising). The third method aims to increase the effective range of the organisation by entering new segments in the market and making products accessible to consumers within these segments (Jeannet & Hennessey, 2001:686).

2) Market share growth

Where market expansion tries to increase the number of transactions of consumers, the market share growth aims is to increase the proportion of sales that are made by the organisation in a specific market, which is relative to a competitor's market share, usually by convincing consumers to buy from the organisation instead of its competitors. This is perceived as a rather hostile strategy (Jeannet & Hennessey, 2001:688).

3) Niche market

The niche market strategy aims to firmly secure a section of the market, which usually consists of a smaller market share, by projecting a different perception of a product to consumers in comparison to other organisations (Jeannet & Hennessey, 2001:689).

4) Status quo

This strategy aims to maintain the proportion of the market by making sure that the organisation's consumers are satisfied every year (Jeannet & Hennessey, 2001:690).

5) Market exit

The market exit strategy seeks to remove a product that is of no substantial benefit to the organisation, by convincing another organisation to purchase it or simply by eliminating the product from the range of commodities that are offered (Jeannet & Hennessey, 2001:690).

ii. Growth market share matrix

Figure 3.3 illustrates the growth market share matrix. The vertical axis represents the growth rate of business in percentages and the horizontal axis represents the relative market share of the four quadrants.

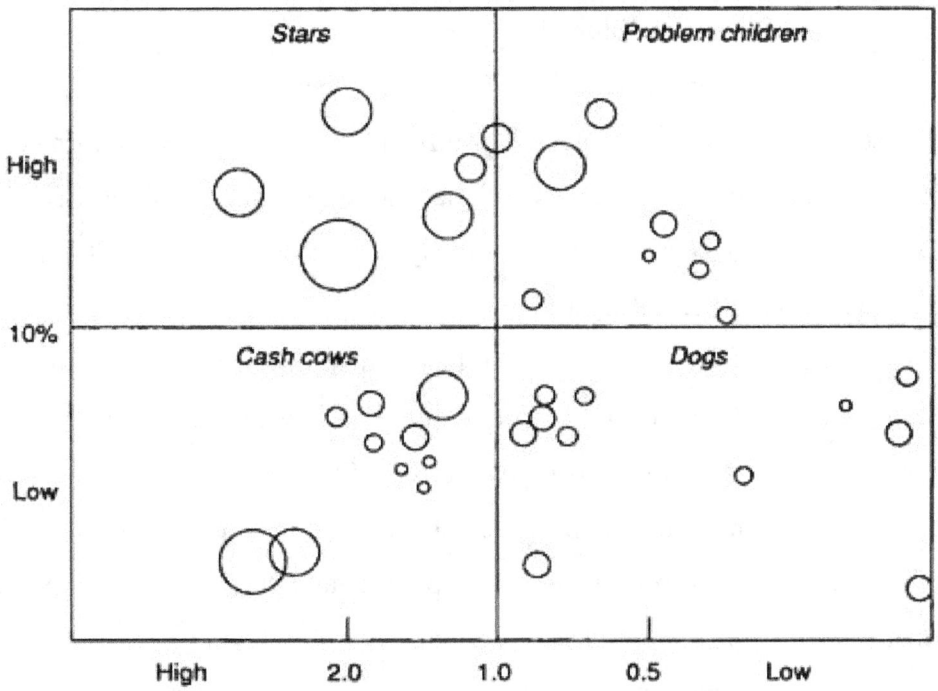

Figure 3.3: Growth market share matrix: Product portfolio chart (O'Shaughness, 1995:50)

The relationship between market share and the market growth rate are depicted in
The four quadrants delineate four types of products/businesses namely:

1) *Stars* are high-growth businesses or products competing in markets in which they are relatively strong compared with the competition. They often need investment to sustain their growth. Eventually, their growth will slow down and, assuming they maintain their relative market share, they become "cash cows."

2) *Cash* cows are low-growth businesses or products with a relatively high market share. These are mature, successful businesses with relatively little need for investment. They need to be managed for continued profit so that they continue to generate the strong cash flows that the company needs for its "stars."

3) *Problem children* are businesses or products with low market share that operate in higher-growth markets. This suggests that they have potential but may require a substantial investment to grow market share at the expense of more powerful competitors.

4) *Dogs* refer to businesses or products that have low relative share in unattractive, low-growth markets. Dogs may generate enough cash to break even, but they are rarely ever worth investing in (O'Shaughness, 1995:51).

iii. Marketing influences on consumer decision-making

Marketing strategies are often designed to influence consumer decision-making and lead to profitable exchanges. Each element of the marketing mix (product, price, promotion, and place) can affect consumers in different ways (Peter & Donnelly, 2004:45).

1. Product influences

Several attributes of an organisation's products, including brand name, quality, newness and complexity, can affect consumer behaviour. The physical appearance of the product, packaging and labelling information can also influence whether consumers notice a product in-store, examine it and purchase it. One of the key tasks of marketers is to differentiate their products from those of competitors and create consumer perceptions that the product is worth purchasing (Doyle & Stern, 2006:87-98).

2. Price influences

The price of products and services often influences whether consumers will purchase them at all and, if so, which competitive offering is selected. Stores such as Pick 'n Pay are perceived to charge low prices and attract consumers based on this fact alone. For some offerings, higher prices may not deter purchase because consumers believe that the products or services are of a higher quality or are more prestigious. However, many value-conscious consumers may buy products more on the basis of price rather than other attributes (Peter & Donnelly, 2004:55).

3. Promotion influences

Advertising, sales promotions, salespeople and publicity can influence consumer's perceptions of products, what emotions they experience when purchasing and using them, and what behaviours they display, including shopping in particular stores and purchasing specific brands. Since consumers receive so much information from marketers and screen out a good deal of it, it is important for marketers to devise communications that (1) offer consistent messages about their products; and (2) are placed in media that consumers in the target market are likely to use. Marketing communications play a critical role in informing consumers about products and services, including where they can be purchased, and in creating favourable images and perceptions (Doyle & Stern, 2006:89).

4. Place influences

The marketer's strategy for distributing products can influence consumers in several ways. First, products that are convenient to buy in a variety of stores increase the chances of consumers to find and buy them. When consumers seek low-involvement products, they are unlikely to engage in extensive search, hence the need for product availability in stores.

Second, consumers may perceive products that are sold in exclusive outlets as being of a higher quality. In fact, one of the ways in which marketers create brand equity that is favourable in terms of consumer perceptions of brands, is by selling them in prestigious outlets. Third, offering products via non-store methods such as on the Internet or in catalogues can create consumer perceptions that the products are innovative, exclusive, or tailored for specific target markets (Doyle & Stern, 2006:95).

Psychological influences on consumer decision-making

Information from several groups, marketing and situational influences affects what consumers think and feel about particular products and brands. However, there are a number of psychological factors that influence how this information is interpreted and used, and how it impacts the consumer decision-making process. Two of the most important psychological factors are product knowledge and product involvement (Peter & Donnelly, 2004:58).

Product knowledge

Product knowledge refers to the amount of information that a consumer has stored in her or his memory about particular product classes, product forms, brands, models and ways to purchase them. For example, a consumer may be more informed about wine in respect of type (product class); red or white wine (product form); Tall Horse versus Groot Constantia (brand); and various package sizes (models) and stores that sell it (ways to purchase).

Group marketing and situational influences determine the initial level of product knowledge, as well as changes. For example, a consumer may hear about a new wine shop opening from a friend (group influence), see an advert for it in the newspaper (marketing influence), or see the shop on the way to work (situational influence). Any of these influences would increase the amount of product knowledge; in this case a new source for purchasing the product (Peter & Donnelly, 2004:59).

5. Retail Operations

The philosophy of operating retail stores is to serve the customer. This means that a retailer should be the purchasing agent for the customer rather than the distributing agent for the manufacturer. Therefore, the store merchandise should be purchased that customers want rather than the merchandise that the manufacturer wants the retailer to carry. Retailers that can satisfy their customer needs assure themselves as a greater probability of success. Harris and Walters (1992) have classified the various tasks involved in retail operations. Their work with a former director of Tesco has led to the development of a positioning for profit model specifically for use by retailers (Harris & Walter, 1992). Their work identifies the functional strategies that make up the model:

1. Merchandise;
2. Customer service;
3. Trading format and store environment; and

4. Customer communications.

Many studies of small retailers and, in particular, independently owned companies have become the focus for recent work. For instance, Megick (2001) identified six retail operations clusters in his analysis:

1. Merchandise And Range;
2. Service And Quality Lines;
3. Active Marketing;
4. Low Price And Incentives;
5. Local Involvement; And
6. Unique Products.

Archer and Taylor (1994) provide ten survival strategies for small retailers to consider in competing with mega-discount chains. These precepts are (Archer & Taylor, 1994):

1. Focus Completely On Satisfying the Customers;
2. Study the Success of Others;
3. Gather and Analyze Management Information Regularly;
4. Sharpen Marketing Skills;

The initial level of product knowledge may influence how much information is sought when deciding to make a purchase. For example, if a consumer already believes that Groot Constantia wine is the best-tasting wine, knows where to buy it, and knows how much it costs, the consumer will not feel the need to look elsewhere for further information.

Finally, product knowledge influences how quickly a consumer goes through the decision-making process. For example, when purchasing a new product of which the consumer has little product knowledge, extensive information may be sought and more time may be devoted to the decision (Pride & Ferrell, 2010:320).

According to McGee and Finney (1997) distinctive competencies is a particular instrument that can increase an SMR's competitive advantage. More importantly, they suggested that there are five factors in the area of distinctive competence. These are:

1. Quality Image;
2. Effective Differentiation;
3. Effectiveness of Key Merchandising Practices;
4. Civic Involvement; And

5. Control of Retail Program.

   5. Increase the Customer's Perception of Value;

   6. Position the Business Uniquely;

   7. Eliminate Waste;

   8. Find Something to Improve Every Day;

   9. Embrace Change with a Positive Attitude;

   10. Pull The Trigger And Start The Battle.

McGee and Finney (1997) also emphasized that certain areas of distinctive competence do in fact serve as viable sources of competitive advantage for small retailers. In other words, there is a positive correlation between better performance and possession of specific distinctive capabilities or competencies, namely effective merchandising practices and a superior ability to control overall retail program activities.

More recent research has focused on strategies for small independent retailers as a whole as opposed to specifically rural retailers (A. Smith & Sparks, 2000). Jussila et al. (1992) in their study of retail strategies in rural Finland, identify three strategic directions available to retailers, namely 'adaptation', (i.e. operating as effectively as possible with in the prevailing, often hostile, market conditions), 'diversification' (i.e. expanding product ranges and/or offering other services in order to maintain or increase market share in what may be declining market), and 'expansion', (i.e. increasing the number of customers apparently through a focus on attracting custom from tourist visitors to the locality). According to Ansoff (1987), cited in Byrom et, al., (2003), the need for a 'common thread' between the present and future direction of the business, through the specification of what he termed the growth vector. This indicates the direction in which the firm is moving with respect to its current product-market positioning (which, of course, will be influenced by such factors as, for example, the firm's objectives, management preferences, its competences and previous strategic decisions). The frame work developed to illustrate this was the Ansoff matrix, using the dimensions of product and market, as shown in Figure 3.4

Figure 3.4 **The Ansoff matrix with indicative retail strategies**

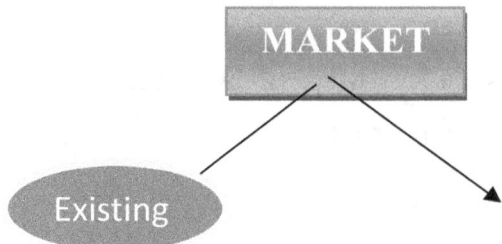

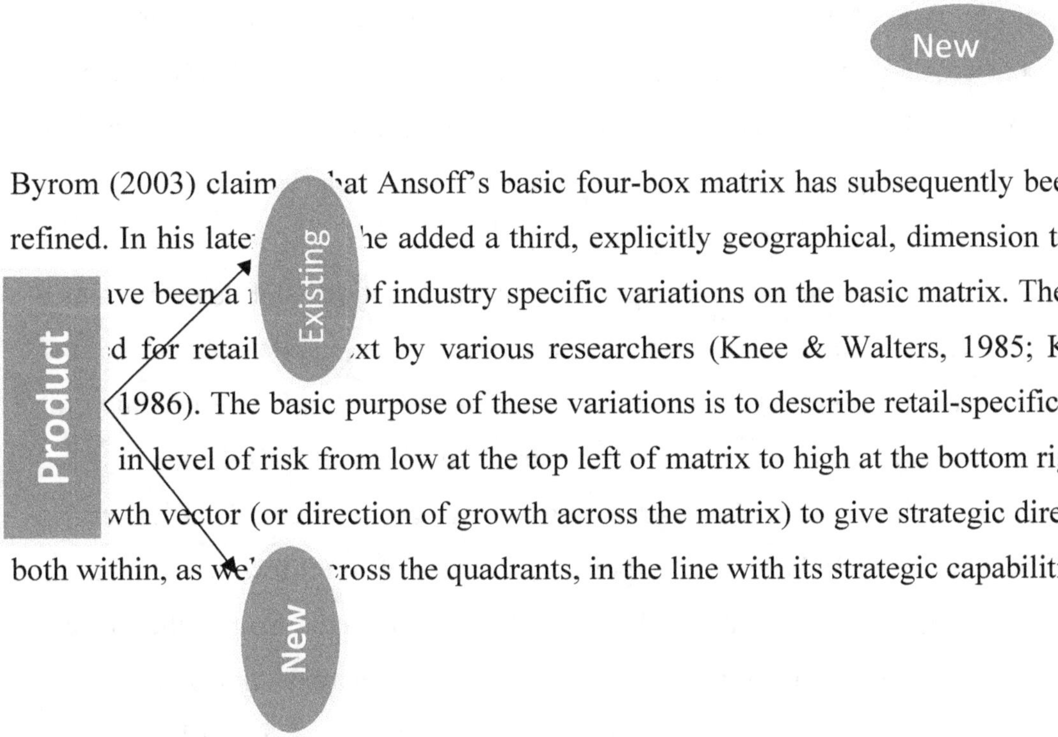

Byrom (2003) claims that Ansoff's basic four-box matrix has subsequently been developed and refined. In his later work, he added a third, explicitly geographical, dimension to the matrix, and have been a number of industry specific variations on the basic matrix. The matrix has been used for retail context by various researchers (Knee & Walters, 1985; Kristenson, 1983; (1986). The basic purpose of these variations is to describe retail-specific strategy options, in level of risk from low at the top left of matrix to high at the bottom right, coupled with with vector (or direction of growth across the matrix) to give strategic direction to the firm, both within, as well as across the quadrants, in the line with its strategic capabilities.

CHAPTER IV
PROFILE OF KOLHAPUR DISTRICT

1 Introduction:

Kolhapur City (16� 42' N; 74" 14' E, Ht. 1870 ft.: 25.7 Sq. miles; p. 1,36,835), stands on rising ground on the south bank of the river Pancaganga, bounded on the north by the Panchganga river, on the east by the boundaries of Uchgaon village, on the south by the boundaries of Kalambe and Pachgaon villages and on the west by the boundaries of Nave palinge, Padali and Singnapur villages and by the Panchganga river.

Climate and Rainfall.

Except from March to May when it is hot, the climate is temperate and healthy. From March to May hot winds prevail, but the sea breeze which begins in the afternoon makes the evenings cool and pleasant. Often, when the heat becomes very oppressive, there is a shower in the evening which brings down the temperature immediately.

Importance.

Kolhapur derives its importance from its past political associations and its position as a great commercial, religious and educational centre. It was the capital of the former Kolhapur State", a premier state in the Deccan, and was also the seat of the Residency for Deccan States. Its importance as a commercial centre is well known. Kolhapur is a big market for jaggery (*Gul*) of which the district is a very large producer. This jaggery is supplied to various parts of India and is exported to different countries. As a religious centre, Kolhapur is known as the Dakshin Kashi or the Kashi of the South, the ancient temple of Mahalakshmi being the main attraction. The city has two Arts and Science Colleges, one Law College, one B. T. College and one Commerce College. It has also 20 High Schools. There are numerous cheap hostel facilities. Kolhapur has produced many well-known artists and sculptors and it has also been the birth place of Marathi film industry. It has been a sports centre and has produced many well-known wrestlers, cricketers and sportsmen who have represented India in international contests. Although mainly a residential and commercial town till lately, Kolhapur is now fast becoming an industrial town with emphasis on the engineering industry.

History

Kolhapur, or as it seems to have been formerly called Karvir, is probably one of the oldest religious and trade centers in western India. In Brahmapuri Hill, near the centre of the present city, have been found Buddhist coins which are believed to belong to the first century before Christ; a small crystal casket which is believed to have enclosed Buddhist relics of about the same age and a shattered model of a brass relic-shrine or daghoba whose shape also belongs to about the first century before Christ. [Jour, B.B.R.A.S. XIV, 147-154.] The discovery of a Shatakarni inscription probably of the first century after Christ at Banavasi in North Kanara and the known extent of the power of that dynasty in the North Deccan, make it probable that, as suggested by Professor Bhandarkar, Ptolemy's (A.D. 150)

Hippokurh rejia Baleokuri refers to Kolhapur, the capital of king Vilvayakura, who from inscriptions is believed to have reigned about A.D. 150.

Recent excavations at Brahmapuri have revealed that " a city of well-built brick houses stood on the banks of the *Pancaganga* river, when the Satvahana (or Audhra according to the Puranas) Emperor, Gautamiputra Satkarni ruled in the Deccan about A.D. 106-130. The beginnings of this city were probably laid in the preceding one or two centuries. [H.D. Sankalia and M. G. Dixit:-Excavations at Brahmapuri (Kolhapur) 1945-46.] "Before the temple of Mahalaksmi was built in the 7th or 8th century there appears to have been six centers of habitation or hamlets. These were, (1) Brahmapuri where though the old city had declined, people continued to live, (2) Uttareshwar, which was a suburb of the old Brahmapuri city, (3) Kholkhandoba which also was a suburb of the old Brahmapuri city, (4) Rankala which seems to have been a separate hamlet, (5) Padmala on the banks of Padmala lake and (6) Ravnesvar which was a separate hamlet. These six centers continued their separate existence up till the building of the Mahalakshmi temple, which became the centre of Kolhapur city. [Kolhapur Nagarpalika-Centenary Souvenir-pp. 174-180,] In former times this great temple was surrounded by a circle of shrines several of which lie buried many feet underground. Every pool of standing water was sacred and in the city and country round about there are many broken images of Brahman and Jain worship which are supposed to belong to temples destroyed by the Musalmans in the thirteenth and fourteenth centuries. According to Major Graham [Graham's Kolhapur, 112.] in the eighth or ninth century an earthquake overturned many temples and buildings in Kolhapur. Among the traces of the earthquake are the two underground temples of Khandoba and Kartik Swami, over which houses have since been built In the old temple of Ambabai the wall is of unequal height in different places, and the ground has passed through so many changes that the original level cannot be discovered. In digging the foundations of the high school in 1870, and in making other excavations, at a depth of over fifteen feet, stones slabs covered with strange figures, shrines and old inscriptions were found. In support of his statement that many of these changes are due to the action of an earthquake Major Graham refers [Graham's Kolhapur 317.] to several small mounds or upheavings near the city and to the discovery in 1849 of the bed of the Panchaganga seventy feet above the level of the present bed. In the Karavir or Kolhapur Mahatmya [Though it probably embodies old legends and traditions the Karvir Mahatmya or the Greatness of Kolhapur wag -written as late as 1730,] or account of the greatness of Kolhapur, Kolhapur is mentioned as the Kashi or Benares of the South. According to local tradition, when the Jains were building the temple of Ambabai on Brahmapuri hill a fort was made by a Kshatri Raja Jaysing who held his court at Bid about nine miles west of Kolhapur. In the twelfth century the Kolhapur fort was the scene of a battle between the Kalahhurya or Kalachurya who had conquered the Kalyani Chalukyas and become the ruler of the Deccan, and the Silaharas of Kolhapur, the feudatories of the Chalukyas. Bhoja Raja II (1178-1209) of the Kolhapur Silaharas made Kolhapur his capital but the headquarters of the State were soon after moved to Panhala about twelve miles to the North-west, and remained there till the country passed to the Bahamani Kings. The Bahamani Sultan Allaudin Hasan Bahmon Shah (1347-1359) towards the end of his reign made a conquest of Goa and Dabhol and while returning from this campaign passed through Karad and Kolhapur where he establihed the rule of the muslims. Kolhapur is next mentioned as the place where Mahmudd Gawan (1469) encamped during rainy season in his expedition against Vishalgad. [Briggs Ferishta, II., 482-485,] Under the Bijapur Kings, from 1489 till it came under Shivaji about 1659, owing to its nearness to the strong fort of Panhala, a Bijapur Officer was stationed at Kolhapur. Under the Marathas, especially after 1730, when it became independent of Satara, Kolhapur rose in importance. In 1782 the seat of Government was moved from Panhala to Kolhapur. Up to this time Kolhapur's only protection against robbers and enemies was a mud wall. During the feuds between the Patvardhans and the Kolhapur State (1773-1810) which filled the latter years of the eighteenth century, a stone wall thirty feet high and ten to twenty-six feet thick, was built more than 1� miles in circumference. At equal distances the wall had

forty-five bastions with battlements and loopholes and outside a deep and wide ditch with a rough glacis. In the wall were six gateways, three of them with stout wooden gates, bristling with long iron spikes to keep off elephants. After the river reservoirs and the wards to which they led, the gates were named the Ganga, Rahkala, Varunitirth, Aditvar, Mangalvar and Sanivar, The entrance to each gate was across a drawbridge. The gates used to be shut at eleven in the evening and opened by four in, the morning. [With four of the six gates some great event is connected. By the Ganga gate which opened on the Panchaganga River, no corpse except one of a member of the royal family was allowed to be carried. By the Aditvar gate, in 1857 the second band of rebels led by Firangu Shinda entered the town, broke into the jail, and set the prisoners free. By the Mangalvar gate, in 1857 the rebels of the 27th Kolhapur Native Infantry tried in vain to enter the city. At the Shanvar gate, which is said to have been built by Ali Adil Shah I of Bijapur (1557-1579), a hard battle was fought in 1800 between the Raja of Kolhapur and the Patwardhans under Ramchandra, son of the well known Parshurambhau. In this gate, after a siege of two months a breach was made scaling ladders were applied, and the city was on the point of being taken when an intrigue at the Poona Court suddenly obliged the assailants to leave the city. In 1858 by breaking open the Shanvar gate, Sir Le Grand Jacob entered the city and arrested the rebels under Firangu Shinda, who was shot by the treasury guard of the Kolhapur infantry.] When the town was growing in the eighteenth century, the people built houses without any order wherever sites could be had, and the streets were narrow, often not broad enough for two carts to pass. As the city increased in size weekly markets came to be held outside the walls. Beyond the walls ten subrubs or *peths* were founded. After the names of the founders or of the presiding god of the place, or of the days on which weekly markets were held, the new suburbs were called Ravivar Somvar, Mangalvar, Budhvar, Sukravar and Sanivar and Uttresvar, Candresvar, Kesapur and Logmapur. In these suburbs the lanes were wide and were planted here and there with trees. In the eighties of the nineteenth century to improve the air and health of the city the walls were pulled down and the ditch filled.

The modern development of Kolhapur can be said to have started when the British obtained political suzerainty in 1844 and built the Residency during 1845-48. The New Palace was built near the Residency in 1877. The chiefs and *jagirdars* also began building their mansions in this area. Then came the railway in 1891-92. The site for the station was selected beyond the Jayantinala, about 2 miles from the city. The station exerted a considerable pull on the city and development of the city towards the station started. The Sahupuri colony was started near the station in 1895 and was completed in 1920. Then came the Laxmipuri colony in 1926-27 between Shahupuri and the city. In 1929, the Rajarampuri Colony was started. In 1933, the area between the railway line and Rajarampuri was developed and was called the Sykes Extension. In the city, fields and vacant sites came to be developed as population increased. From 1884, efforts were made to fill up the numerous lakes and tanks in the city. The Kapiltirth was first filled up and a vegetable market was established on the site. Indrakund was also filled up. The Mahar *talao* Kumbhar *talao,* Umak, Petala, Maskuti, and Ravneswar, were gradually filled up. Khasbag, Sakoli, Varunitirth, Ravanesvar, Belbag, Udyam-nagar and Maskuti *talao* areas came to be developed into residential areas all of which except Khasbag and Sakoli are very recent development, i.e., of 1944-45 onwards.

Wards.

Kolhapur City is divided into five wards. The area comprised in each ward is as follows: -

Ward.	Localities included.
A	Rankala lake, Padmaraje Garden areas, Cattle market, Sakoli area, Kapiltirth area, Babujamal Darga area, Gavataci Mandai, Varuntirth area, Ubha Maruti area, Phirangai area.
B	Mahalaxmi Temple, Khasbag, Palace Theatre, Sathamari, Old Palace, Rajaram, College area, Gujari, Subhasa Cauk, Old Race Course, Subhasa Nagar, Jawahar Nagar, Sambhaji Nagar, Kalamba Jail.
C	Municipal Office, Shivaji Market, Bindu Cauk, Town Hall, Laxmipuri, Gujari, Akbar Mohalla, Sandhya Talkies area, Thorla Maharvad.
D	Gangaves, Sahu Udhyan area, Padmaraje Vidyalaya area, Brahmapuri area, Uttaresvar, Shukravar Peth.
E	Sahupuri, Rajarampuri, Sykes Extension, Tarabai Park area, Temblaivadi, Jadhawadi, Bhosalevadi, Kasba Bavada, Kadamvadi.

Table No 4.1 The number of properties and their annual letting value

The number of properties and their annual letting value is as follows: -

Ward.	No. of properties.	Annual letting value.
A	3,690	8,76,450
B	3,274	7,97,601
C	3,226	16,00,114
D	2,909	6,97,837

| E | 4,521 | 21,52,653 |
| Total | 17,620 | 61,24,655 |

4.1.5 Area and Population.

In 1957 the total limits of the Kolhapur Municipal Borough covered 25.7 square miles. The total population according to the 1951 census was 1, 36,835 of which 71,360 were males and 65,475 females. According to their livelihood the population was distributed as follows: -

Table 4.2 Area and Population According to their livelihood

Agricultural classes-		
	Males.	Females.
(i) Cultivators, cultivating laborers and their dependents.	5,681	4,881
(ii) Non-cultivating owners of land, rent receivers and their dependents.	3,138	3.285
Non-agricultural classes-		
(Persons-including dependents) who derive their principal means of livelihood from-		

Table 4.3 Area and Population According to their languages spoken

	Males.	Females.
(i) Production other than cultivation.	15,945	14,056
(*ii*) Commerce	12,404	11,705
(*iii*) Transport	3,285	2,760
(*iv*) Other services and miscellaneous sources.	30,967	28,788
	62,601	57,309

The distribution of the population according to the languages spoken [Mother tongue.] was as follows:-

Marathi-1,16,702; Kannada-3,687; Urdu-11,773; Gujarati- 1,890; Telugu-1,011; Sindhi-150; Hindi-494; Rajasthani--49.1; Konkani-103; Tamil-301; Hindustani-3; Kacchi-70; Portuguese-7; Tulu-24; Malayalam-39; Punjabi-13; English-35; Naipali-13; Bengali-16; Pashto-5; Chinese-6; Persian-1; Oriya-1.

The population of the Kolhapur Municipal area is distributed as follows according to the religious they profess; Hindus- 1,18,223; Muslims-12,232; Jains-4,809; Christians-1,538; Zoroastrians-15; Buddhists-14; Sikhs-4.

2 History of Kolhapur City.

The civic affairs of Kolhapur City are managed by the Kolhapur Municipal Borough. The beginnings of municipal administration can be traced back to 1830 when the Chatrapati ordered the setting up of an organisation to sweep the roads and to recover the cost by the levy of a tax on houses. In 1850, the Government of India decided to establish municipalities in various towns, and the Resident of Kolhapur formed in 1854 a Municipal Committee for Kolhapur consisting of six members- two officials and four non-officials. A grant of Rs. 3,000 was made for its expenditure. In 1869, instead of the Government grant, certain items of income viz., octroi, *pankhoti*, tobacco tax, fish *makta*, snuff *makta*, bhang and opium *makta*, lease of space in the moat were handed over to the municipality with a view to increasing its income. In 1871, the number of members of the committee was increased to 30. A house-tax was levied in 1873. The Assistant Political Agent was made the President of the municipality and its General Body met every quarter. The actual work was supposed to be done by the Managing Committee but as it was found that the committee was not working satisfactorily, all powers were vested in the President in 1875. From 1881, however, the General Body was being called and quarterly accounts were presented to it. In 1884, there was a move in Bombay Province to have Local Self-Government. This had repercussions in Kolhapur also and in 1886 a committee was appointed to reconstitute the Municipality.

In 1889, the Kolhapur Municipal Rules were framed. According to these Rules, the municipality was to consist of ex-officio members and members appointed by Government, the number of appointed members being at least double that of ex-officio members. From 1904 to 1920, the municipality was suspended due to unsatisfactory working and all powers were vested in the Administrator. In 1920, the municipality was reconstituted with 47 constituencies and caste-wise electorates and it came into office in 1921. Matters, however, did not improve and in 1924, it was again dissolved. In 1925, the Kolhapur State Municipal Act, 1925, modeled on the lines of the Bombay District Municipal Act, 1901, was enacted. The municipality was to have 40 members of whom 20 were appointed by Government and 20 were elected. The first body under this Act was formed in 1926. In 1944, the Kolhapur Municipal Boroughs Act, 1944, was prepared on the lines of the Bombay Municipal Boroughs Act, 1925, and it was applied to the Kolhapur municipality in the same year. The municipality continued under this Act until the merger of the Kolhapur State with Bombay in 1949.

Growth of Municipal Area.

The area of the municipality has increased considerably since its formation. In 1844, it is said to have exceeded four and half square miles and in 1874 it is mentioned as 1,132 acres 29 gunthas. Additions were made to the area from time to time and in 1957 it measured 25.7 square miles.

Constitution.

The Kolhapur municipality has been constituted under the Bombay Municipal Boroughs Act, 1925 as amended from time to time. All the councilors are elected on adult franchise and the total number of seats is 44, of which 37 are general, three are reserved for Scheduled Castes and four for women. The city is divided into 12 constituencies. The distribution of seats according to ward's is as follows:-

Table No 4.4 Constitution : Distribution of seats according to wards

No. of Ward.	Name of Ward.	Total No. of seats.	Seats reserved for Scheduled Castes.	Seats reserved for Women.
1	2	3	4	5
I	A Ward	4	--	--
II	A Ward	4	1	To rotate in Wards I and II beginning with Ward II.
III	B Ward	4	--	--
IV	B Ward	4	1	To rotate in Wards IV and III beginning with Ward IV.
V	C Ward	4	--	--
VI	C and a small	4	--	1

	portion of D.			
VII	D Ward	4	--	--
VIII	D and a small portion of A.	4	1	To rotate in Wards VIII and VII beginning with Ward No. VIII.
IX	E Ward	3	--	1
X	E Ward	3	--	--
XI	E Ward	3	1	To rotate in Wards XI and X beginning with Ward No. XI.
XII	E Ward	3	--	1
--	--	44	4	3

Figure 4.1 Kolhapur District Profile

3 District Profile:

Kolhapur is located in southern part of Maharashtra and is spread through ranges of Sahyadri. The geographical spread of the district is of 7746.40 Sq. K.ms. The city of Kolhapur is the district head quarter. The administration of the district is governed through four Revenue Sub Divisions, 12 Tehasils and 12 Panchayat Samittees.

Sub -Division Tehsils Covered

a) Karveer, Panhala, Kagal , Shahuwadi

b) Ichalkaranji, Shirol, Hatkanangle

c) Gadhinglaj, Ajara, Chandgad, Gadhinglaj

d) Radhanagari, Bhudargad, Radhanagari, Gaganbawada

Three types of soils are found in the district viz. Red laterite soil in Western Hilly Area, River bed deep soil in central part of the district and medium to heavy black soil in Eastern Part of the District. The district receives rainfall ranging from 1000 mm. to 4680 mm. with average rainfall of 2015 mm. The land admeasuring 140781 hectares is covered with forest. The district is blessed with 7 main perennial rivers viz. Krishna, Warana, Dudhganga, Vedganga, Hiranyakeshi, Chatprabha and Panchaganga (Kumbhi, Kasari, Tulashi, and Bhogavati). All the rivers flow from West to East. The net irrigated area of the district is 128000 Ha, Which is about 26% of the net area sown which is 476916 Ha. The above mentioned seven prominent rivers and other rivers in the district irrigate about 62% of the net area by Surface water. The main cash crop of the district is sugarcane. Other crops grown in the district includes Paddy, Jawar, Nagli, Wheat, Soyabean, Tur, Gram, Groundnut, 75 Sunflowers, Vegetables, Potato, Tomatoes, and Cashew etc.

CHAPTER V
CUSTOMER'S OPINION ON UNORGANIZED RETAIL

1 Introduction :

1. This Chapter deals with the research results regarding the comparison of Marketing Strategies of small retail houses and large retail houses in Kolhapur city. For a better understanding of the comparison of the Marketing Strategy of the large retail houses and small retail houses Quality of Air Conditioning, Space/chairs for sitting, Household items, Use of Technology, Level of Spaciousness, Child Centered Facilities, Crowd Level, Clothes are identified as the major factors for this study.

TABLE No: 5.2.1

Age of the Respondents (in years)

Sr. No	Age	Frequency	Percent	Valid Percent	Cumulative Percent
1	< 15	10	4.3	4.3	4.3
2	15 - 25	101	43.0	43.0	47.2
3	25 - 35	53	22.6	22.6	69.8
4	35 - 45	37	15.7	15.7	85.5
5	above 45	34	14.5	14.5	100.0
	Total	235	100.0	100.0	

Source: Field Survey 2012

GRAPH No: 5.2.1

Age of the Respondents (in years)

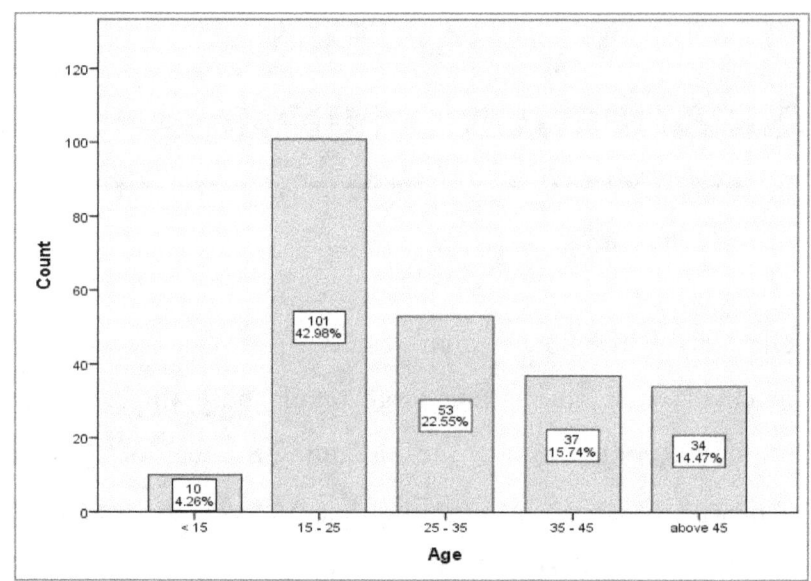

The above table reveals that there are 42.98 % of customers who are between the age group of 15 – 25, 22.55% of the customers are between the age group of 25 – 35, while 15.74 % are within 35 – 45 and 14.47 % are above 45 age group. Only 4.26 % of the customers are below 15 years of age.

Hence it can be interpreted that the highest percentage of customers visiting small retailers lie in the age group of 15-25 followed by the customers of age group 25 -35. It can also be noted that 80% of the customers are in the age group of 15 – 45. This is clearly reflecting that the young generation is mostly visiting the small retailers. It also reinforces the fact that India is a country of youth with an average of 15 – 45 years of age group.

Hence it is suggested to the retailers that the target customer largely lies around 15- 45 years and hence their strategies should be designed so as to attract the tastes and preferences of this lot of customers. Also, the segment to be targeted in terms of age bar is mixed but largely above 15 years.

It can also be concluded that children are not the decision makers in the family to buy grocery.

TABLE No: 5.2.2
Gender of the Respondents.

Sr. No	Gender	Frequency	Percent	Valid Percent	Cumulative Percent
1	Male	165	70.2	70.2	70.2

| 2 | Female | 70 | 29.8 | 29.8 | 100.0 |
| 3 | Total | 235 | 100.0 | 100.0 | |

Source: Field Survey 2012

GRAPH No: 5.2.2
Gender of the Respondents.

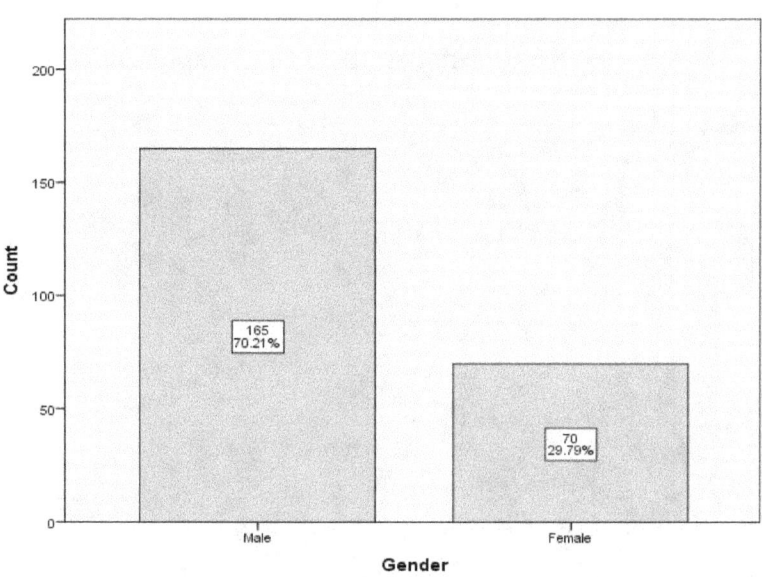

Above table shows that 70.21 % of the respondents visiting the small retail houses are males while 29.79 % of the respondents visiting the small retail houses are females.

Hence we can see that majority of the actual customers who purchase is males. It can be concluded that though India has developed itself in the past since so many decades but it still is a male dominated country.

The decision makers are males even when it comes to basic items like grocery. A good sign which is visible is that in concern to decision making the percentage of females is also slowly on an increasing trend.

It can be suggested to the large retail shop owners that as seen from the above table and graph more attention is to be given to the women buyers as well, as they seem to be on an increasing trend in concern with the decision making.

TABLE No: 5.2.3
Residential Area of the Respondents

	Residential Area	Frequency	Percent	Valid Percent	Cumulative Percent
1	Rural	142	60.4	60.4	60.4

2	Urban	93	39.6	39.6	100.0
	Total	235	100.0	100.0	

Source: Field Survey 2012

GRAPH No: 5.2.3
Residential Area of the Respondents.

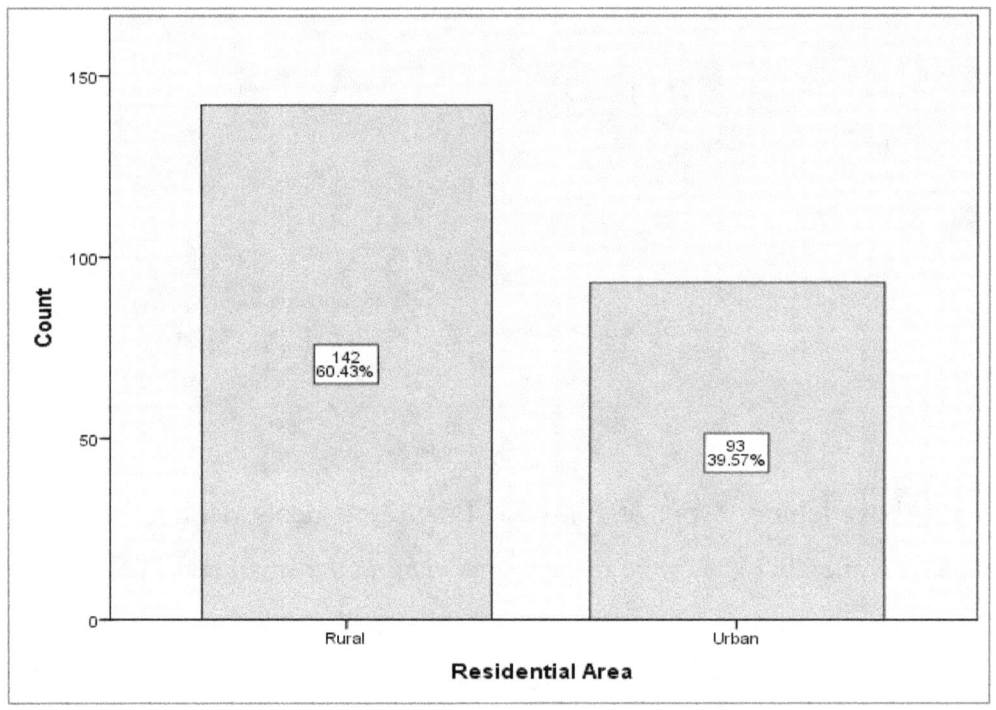

It is reflected by the above table 60.43 % of the respondents purchasing grocery from the small retail houses belong to rural areas while 39.57 % of the respondents visiting the small retail houses are coming from urban areas.

It can be interpreted that majority of the respondents who are buying grocery from small retail shops are from the rural background. Also, it is observed by the researcher that the size of the rural population is growing because of the agricultural income growth in rural part of Kolhapur. The rural market is definitely an opportunity for retailers with an innovative retail proposition.

Hence it is suggested to the small retailers that they should target rural customers by giving them attractive facilities such as credit facilities, free home delivery, availability of products in small quantity etc.

TABLE No: 5.2.4
Marital Status of the Respondents.

Marital Status		Frequency	Percent	Valid Percent	Cumulative Percent
Valid	Married	115	48.9	48.9	48.9
	Unmarried	101	43.0	43.0	91.9
	Single	19	8.1	8.1	100.0
	Total	235	100.0	100.0	

Source: Field Survey 2012

GRAPH No: 5.2.4
Marital Status of the Respondents.

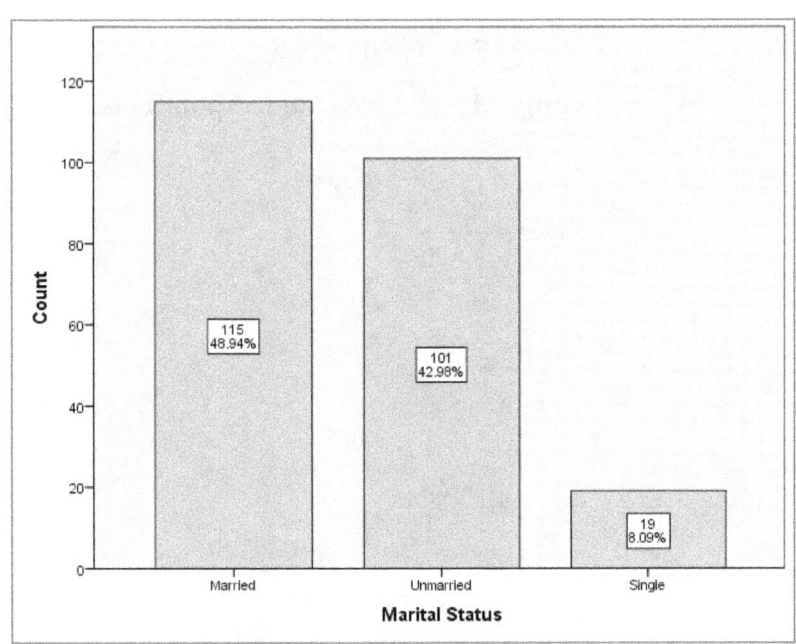

Above table shows that 48.9 % customers visiting the small retail houses are married while 43 % customers visiting small retail shops are unmarried, only in 8.1 % of the customers visiting the small retail houses are single.

It can be construed that percentage of married customers is only slightly higher than the unmarried ones which indicates the requirements of married and unmarried people are equally being catered by the small retailers.

TABLE No: 5.2.5
No. of Family Members of the Respondents.

Sr. No	No. of Family Member	Frequency	Percent	Valid Percent	Cumulative Percent
1	Below 3	34	14.5	14.5	14.5
2	3 – 5	134	57.0	57.0	71.5
3	5 – 7	52	22.1	22.1	93.6
4	More then 7	15	6.4	6.4	100.0
	Total	235	100.0	100.0	

Source: Field Survey 2012

GRAPH No: 5.2.5
No. of Family Members of the Respondents.

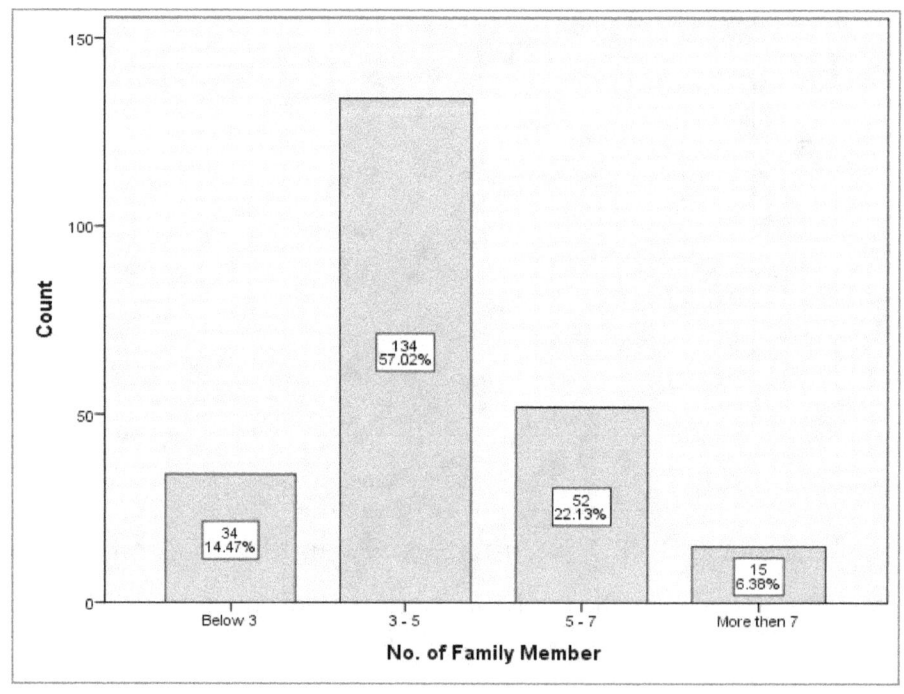

Above graph shows that 14.47 % of the respondents visiting the small retail houses are having less than three family members, 57.02% of customers visiting the small retail houses are having 3 – 5 members in the family, 22.13 % customers visiting the small retail houses are having 5 – 7 members in the family, While, 6.38 % customers visiting the small retail houses are having more than 7 family members in their families.

It is evident from the above graph that majority of the customers who are buying grocery from small retail shops are having the family members up to 3 – 5 in number followed by members up to 5 – 7 in number.

Hence it can be concluded that if number of family members is between 3 – 5 then the customers are getting driven to the small retail houses more number of times.

It can be suggested to the small retailers that a family with 3 – 5 number of members is their target. Simultaneously they should take sincere efforts to attract small families also. Attractive schemes, discount offers on first come basis, gifts for children like toffees, small toys etc. can be considered.

TABLE No: 5.2.6

No. of Children of the Respondents.

	No. of Children	Frequency	Percent	Valid Percent	Cumulative Percent
Valid	Less then 2	48	20.4	20.4	20.4
	2 – 4	85	36.2	36.2	56.6
	> 4	16	6.8	6.8	63.4
	No Children	86	36.6	36.6	100.0
	Total	235	100.0	100.0	

Source: Field Survey 2012

GRAPH No: 5.2.6
No. of Children of the Respondents.

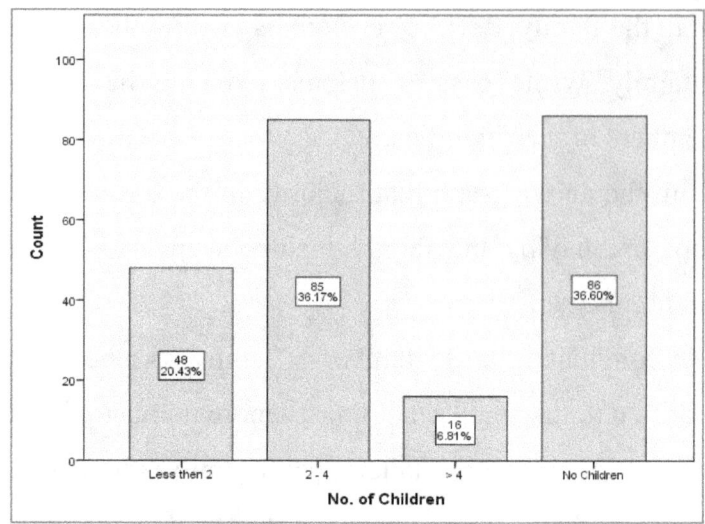

The table given above shows that 20.43 % of the respondents visiting the small retail houses have less than two children in their families, 36.17 % of the respondents visiting the small retail houses have 2 – 4 children in their families, 6.81 % of the respondents visiting the small retail houses possess more than 4 children while 36.6 % of the respondents visiting the small retail houses have no children.

It can hence be construed that the respondents are having approximately equal distribution in the case of 2 – 4 number of children and no children.

Hence we can conclude that the decision to shop in a small retail shop or not is independent of the number of children in the family.

TABLE No: 5.2.7

Education of the Respondents.

	Education	Frequency	Percent	Valid Percent	Cumulative Percent
Valid	0 - 9	11	4.7	4.7	4.7
	10 - 12	35	14.9	14.9	19.6
	Graduate	106	45.1	45.1	64.7
	PG	76	32.3	32.3	97.0
	Any Other	7	3.0	3.0	100.0
	Total	235	100.0	100.0	

Source: Field Survey 2012

GRAPH No: 5.2.7

Education of the Respondents.

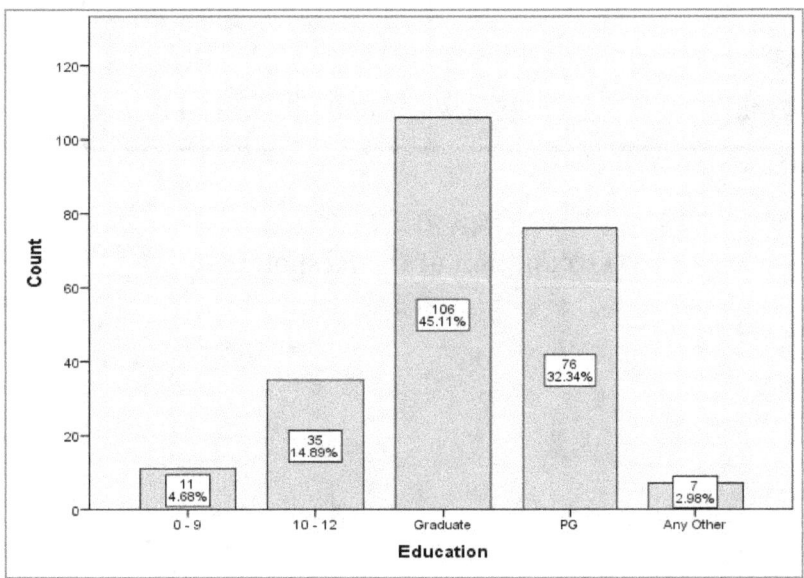

It is reflected by the above table that 4.68 % of customers visiting the small retail houses have completed their education between 0 – 9 standard, 14.89 % of customers visiting the small retail houses have studied between 10 – 12 standard, 45.11 % customers visiting the small retail houses are graduate, 32.3 % customers visiting the small retail houses have completed their Post-Graduation, while only 2.98 % of customers visiting the small retail houses have taken up any other degree in education.

It is evident that majority of customers visiting small retail shop are educated i.e. they have completed their graduation. Also, 32.3 % of the respondents are post graduate. Hence it can be concluded that customers as they are well educated are not taking the decision on emotional basis regarding the shopping in small retail shop rather they are capable of deciding going to small retailers by considering all pros and cons.

It is suggested to the retailers that they should think twice before giving false offers or schemes to the customer. If they will do this then they will definitely lose their customers in their long run.

TABLE No: 5.2.8
Occupation of the Respondents.

Occupation		Frequency	Percent	Valid Percent	Cumulative Percent
Valid	Service	82	34.9	34.9	34.9

	Businessmen	35	14.9	14.9	49.8
	Student	75	31.9	31.9	81.7
	Other	43	18.3	18.3	100.0
	Total	**235**	**100.0**	**100.0**	

Source: Field Survey 2012

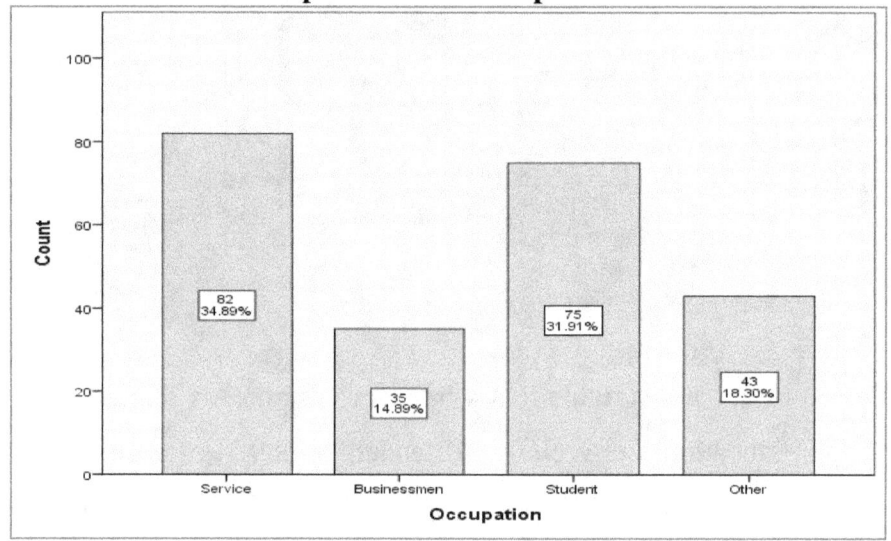

GRAPH No: 5.2.8
Occupation of the Respondents.

The above table displays that 34.9 % of the respondents visiting the small retail houses are doing service, 14.9 % of the respondents visiting the small retail houses are from business background, 31.9 % of the customers visiting the small retail houses are students, While 18.30 % of the customers visiting the small retail houses are from various other occupations.

Hence we can say that the target customers are from different occupations. Majority of the customers are service people followed by students. It can be concluded that as business people do not have enough spare time they are not visiting small retail shops. But they can be good target to small retailers as they have enough disposable income.

It is suggested that considering the shortage of time with the businessmen orders on phone can be taken, home delivery as per their convenient time should be introduced. Opening and closing timings may also be varied as per their spare time.

TABLE No: 5.2.9

Monthly Family Income of the Respondents. (in Rupees)

Monthly Family Income		Frequency	Percent	Valid Percent	Cumulative Percent
Valid	< 5,000	25	10.6	10.6	10.6
	5,000 - 15,000	73	31.1	31.1	41.7
	15,000 - 30,000	82	34.9	34.9	76.6
	30,000 - 45,000	34	14.5	14.5	91.1
	45,000 +	21	8.9	8.9	100.0
	Total	235	100.0	100.0	

Source: Field Survey 2012

GRAPH No: 5.2.9
Monthly Family Income of the Respondents. (in Rupees)

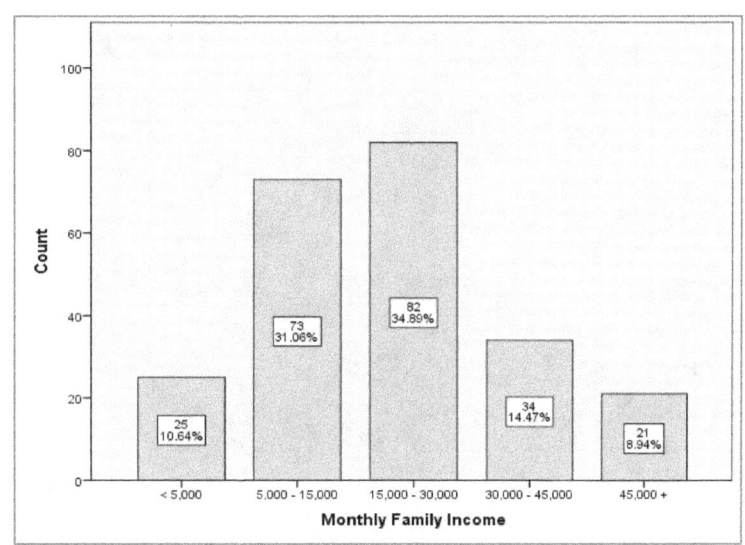

Above graph shows that the monthly family income of 10.64 % customers visiting the small retail shops is < Rs. 5,000/-, the Monthly family income of 31.06 % customers is between Rs. 5,000/- – Rs. 15,000/- , that of 14.47 % customers is between Rs. 30,000/- - Rs. 45,000/-, While 8.94 % of customers are having monthly family income above Rs. 45,000/-.

It can easily be interpreted that the average monthly family income of the customers is ranging from Rs. 5,000/- to Rs. 30,000/- followed by monthly family income of Rs. 30,000/- – Rs. 45,000/- .

Thus we can conclude that this middle income group whose earnings are between Rs. 5,000 to 45,000 has to be chiefly targeted.

TABLE No: 5.2.10

Average Spending per Month on Grocery of the Respondents.

	Average Spending per Month on Grocery	Frequency	Percent	Valid Percent	Cumulative Percent
Valid	< 2,000	41	17.4	17.4	17.4
	2,000 - 4,000	97	41.3	41.3	58.7
	4,000 - 7,000	77	32.8	32.8	91.5
	7,000 +	20	8.5	8.5	100.0
	Total	235	100.0	100.0	

Source: Field Survey 2012

GRAPH No: 5.2.10
Average Spending per Month on Grocery of the Respondents.

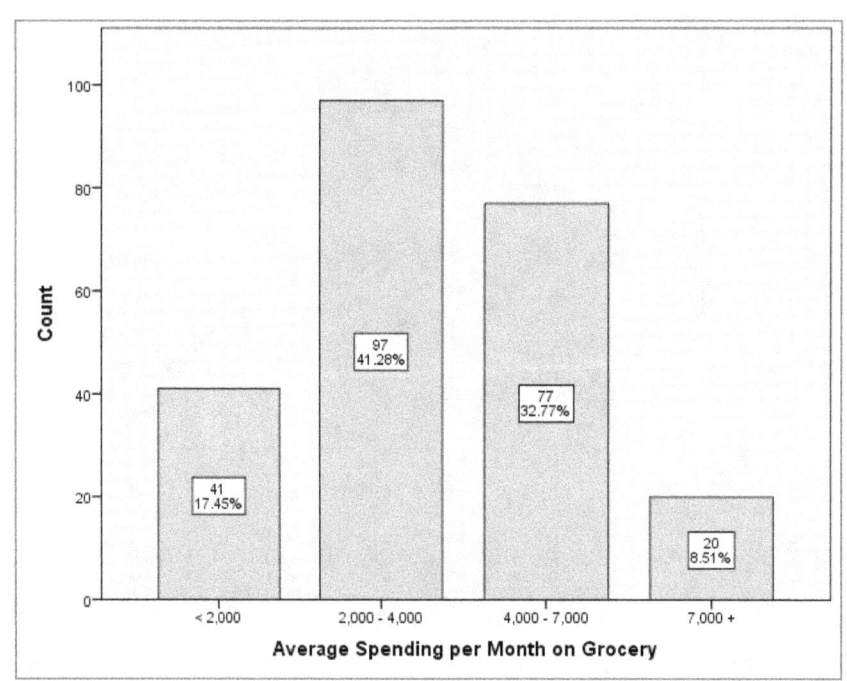

It can be seen from the above table that 17.45 % of respondents visiting the small retail houses are spending less than Rs. 2,000/- per month on grocery, While 41.28 % of customers visiting the small retail houses average spending per month on grocery is between Rs. 2,000/- – Rs. 4,000/-. The average spending per month on grocery is Rs. 4,000/- – Rs. 7,000/- for 32.77 % customers visiting the small retail houses and 8.51 % of customers visiting the small retail houses spend Rs. 7,000/- on an average monthly on grocery.

It can be interpreted that a large amount of customers are spending Rs. 2000/- – Rs. 7000/- on purchasing grocery from the small retail houses.

Hence, it can be concluded that the respondents have trust on the small retailers and they are loyal to them. It is suggested to the retailers that they should try to maintain this trust to retain the customers and to attract the new ones.

TABLE No : 5.2.11
Vehicle Owned by the Respondents.

Own Vehicle		Frequency	Percent	Valid Percent	Cumulative Percent
Valid	Yes	185	78.7	78.7	78.7
	No	50	21.3	21.3	100.0
	Total	**235**	**100.0**	**100.0**	

Source: Field Survey 2012

GRAPH No: 5.2.11
Vehicle Owned by the Respondents.

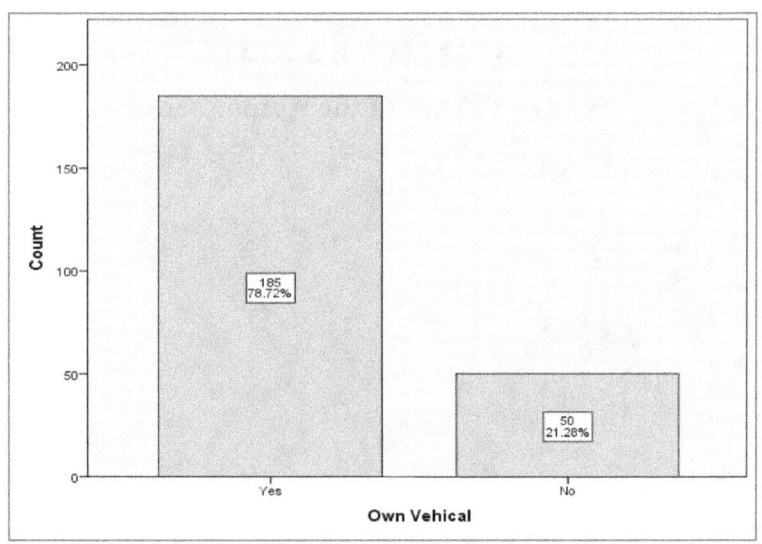

Above Table and graph shows 78.72 % of the customers who visit the small retail shops are having their own vehicle while 21.28 % of the respondents do not possess any vehicle.

It can be observed that majority of the respondents visit the small retailers on their vehicles. It is thus suggested to the retailers that they should have some empty parking space around their shop or have a basement parking zone, so that the customers don't have to waste time in parking it far off. This will cause inconvenience to them and chances are there that the customers will shift to the competitors where enough parking space is available.

Also small retail shopkeepers have to see to it that the parking place is clean enough with a security guards appointed on duty to take care of the vehicles. The parking area can be made use of by flashing hoardings of new arrivals in the shops and making the place more attractive.

TABLE No: 5.2.12

Type of Vehicle of the Respondents.

Type of Vehicle		Frequency	Percent	Valid Percent	Cumulative Percent
Valid	Two Wheeler	134	57.0	66.3	66.3
	Four Wheeler	33	14.0	16.3	82.7
	Both	35	14.9	17.3	100.0
	Total	202	86.0	100.0	
Missing System		33	14.0		
Total		235	100.0		

Source: Field Survey 2012

GRAPH No: 5.2.12

Type of Vehicle of the Respondents.

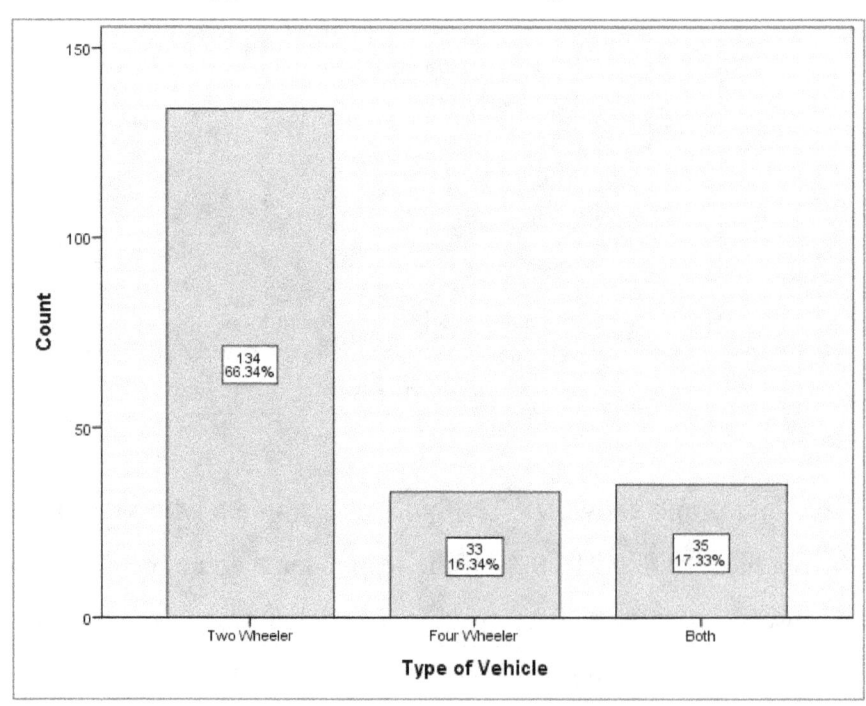

The table given above indicates that 66.34 % of the customers visiting the small retail shop possess a two wheeler, 16.43 % of the customers visiting the small retail houses possess a Four Wheeler and 17.33 % of the customers visiting the small retail houses possess both Two wheeler as well as four wheeler.

Here we can see that majority of customers visiting small retail shops use two wheelers i.e. nearly 70 % of the customers use two wheelers vehicle.

It is suggested to arrange for a comfortable Two Wheeler parking area in and around the small retail houses.

TABLE No: 5.2.13

Frequency of Visiting the Mall by the Respondents.

Frequency of Visiting the Mall		Frequency	Percent	Valid Percent	Cumulative Percent
Valid	Daily	24	10.2	10.2	10.2
	Weekly	71	30.2	30.2	40.4
	Fortnightly	7	3.0	3.0	43.4
	Monthly	69	29.4	29.4	72.8
	As per Need	64	27.2	27.2	100.0
	Total	**235**	**100.0**	**100.0**	

Source: Field Survey 2012

GRAPH No: 5.2.13

Frequency of Visiting the Shop by the Respondents.

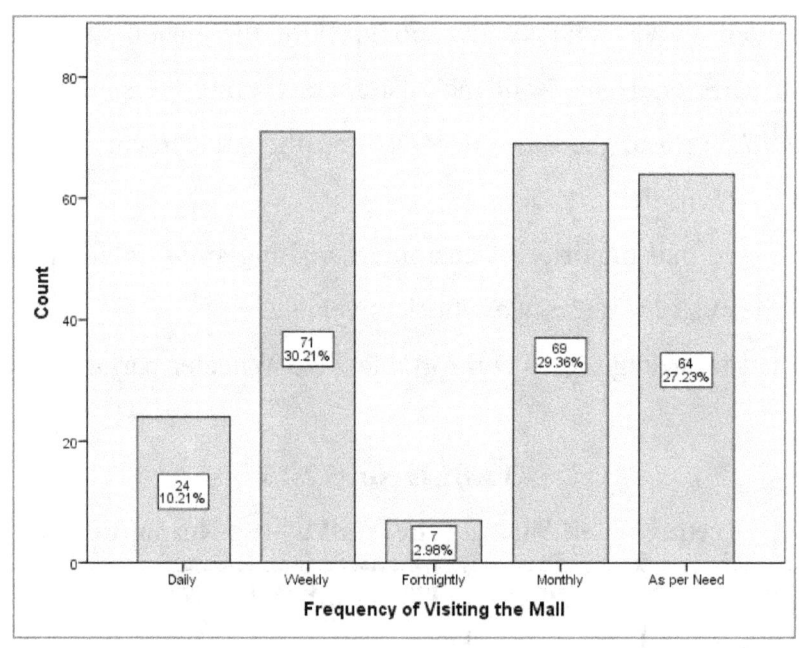

The above graph depicts the frequency of customers visiting the mall. It is visible that 10.21 % of the respondents visit the shop on daily basis, 30.21 % Customers visit the small retail houses on Weekly basis, 2.98 % of the Customers visit the shop on fortnightly basis, 29.36 % of the Customers visit the shop on Monthly basis and 27.23 % of the customers visit the shop as per need.

Hence we can say there is a constant flow of the customers to shop the whole of the month. We cannot say that the customers are visiting only during any specific period like weekdays or beginning of the month.

TABLE No: 5.2.14
Get all the Items in time by the Respondents

Get all the Items in time	Frequency	Percent	Valid Percent	Cumulative Percent
Always	91	38.7	38.7	38.7
Sometimes	133	56.6	56.6	95.3
Never	11	4.7	4.7	100.0
Total	**235**	**100.0**	**100.0**	

Source: Field Survey 2012

GRAPH No: 5.2.14

Get all the Items in time by the Respondents.

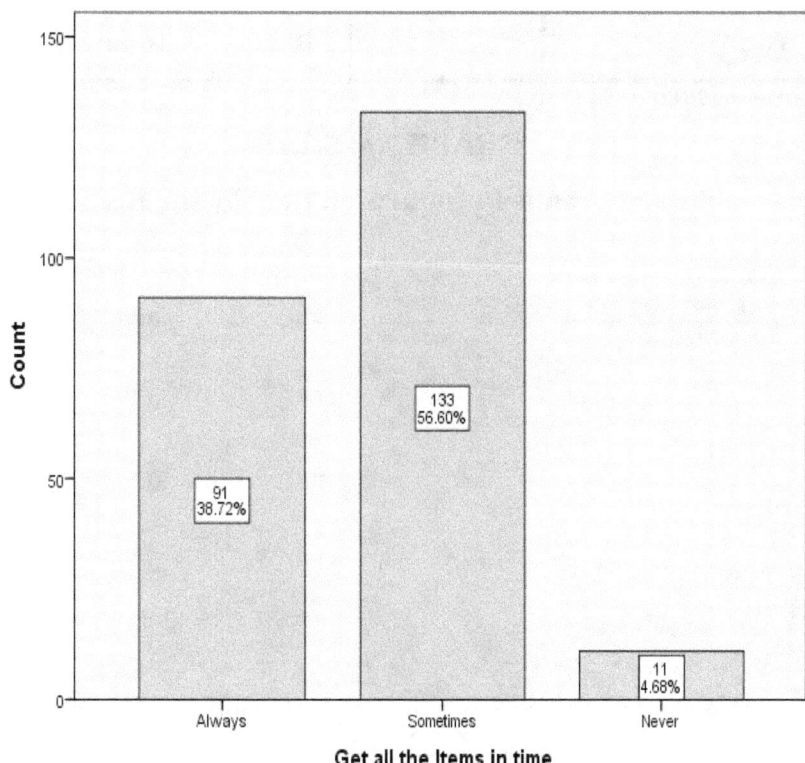

The above table reflects that 56.6 % of the customers visiting the small retail houses of Kolhapur city have responded that they sometimes get all the items needed by them in time followed by 38.72 % of the customers visiting the small retail houses are saying that they always get all the items in time. Only 4.7 % of the customers visiting the small retail houses have responded that they never get all the items in time.

This shows that majority of the respondents are having no complaints regarding the availability of the items in the small retail shops.

TABLE No: 5.2.15

Availability of branded products on time by the Respondents.

Availability of branded products on time	Frequency	Percent	Valid Percent	Cumulative Percent
Valid Always	58	24.7	24.7	24.7

	Sometimes	166	70.6	70.6	95.3
	Never	11	4.7	4.7	100.0
	Total	**235**	**100.0**	**100.0**	

Source: Field Survey 2012

GRAPH No: 5.2.15

Availability of branded products on time by the Respondents.

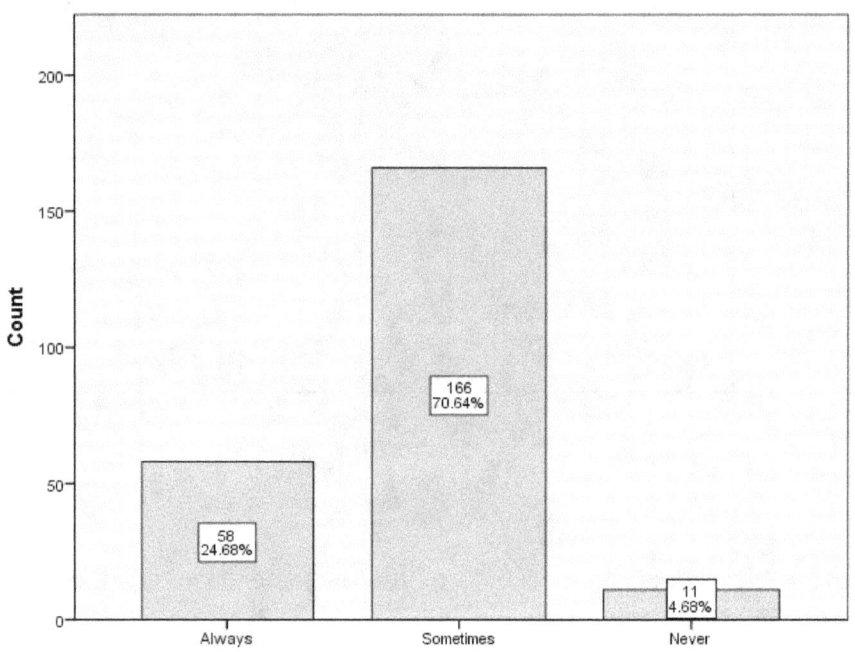

The above table depicts that 24.68 % of the respondents visiting the small retail houses say that the branded products are always available in time with the small retail shops, 70.64 % of the respondents visiting the small retail houses say that they are only sometimes available while 4.68 % of the customers visiting the small retail houses have responded that branded products are never available at the small retail shops.

It can hence be interpreted that small retailers are not much concerned about stocking branded products. Majority of the customers i.e. approximately 75 % are having a strong feeling that they are not getting the branded products at the small retailers. Hence it is necessary that small retail shoppers have to concentrate on making the branded products available on time.

It is suggested to the retailers that they should understand the fact that Kolhapur district is getting urbanized at a very fast pace. The process of globalization has created a strong awareness in the mind of consumers regarding the various brands available for a small product like pencil also. They should keep branded products also in stock so as to retain the customers with them.

TABLE No: 5.2.16
Dealings by the shopkeeper

Dealings by the shopkeeper		Frequency	Percent	Valid Percent	Cumulative Percent
Valid	Highly Fair	31	13.2	13.2	13.2
	Fair	105	44.7	44.7	57.9
	Neutral	86	36.6	36.6	94.5
	Unfair	11	4.7	4.7	99.1
	Highly Unfair	2	.9	.9	100.0
	Total	235	100.0	100.0	

Source: Field Survey 2012

GRAPH No: 5.2.16
Dealings by the shopkeeper

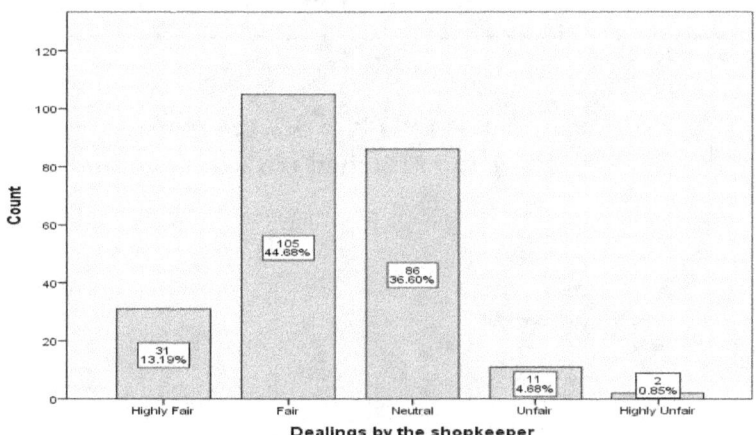

The above table indicates that 13.19 % of the respondents visiting the small retail houses feel that the small retail shopkeepers are highly fair in their dealings with them, 44.68 % of the respondents visiting the small retail houses feel that they are fair, 36.60 % of the customers visiting the small retail houses are neutral about it, 4.68 % of customers visiting the small retail houses responded at dealings by the shopkeeper with the customers are unfair. Only 0.85 % of the customers visiting the small retail houses have responded that the dealings by the shopkeeper are highly unfair.

It can be interpreted that majority of the customers buying from small retail shops are having trust on the small retailers regarding the dealings of the shopkeeper.

Hence, it can be concluded that the small retailers are giving importance to the relationships with the customers. They are trying hard to maintain the trust of the customers in them. The customers also feel that the shopkeepers are fair in their dealings and they trust the shopkeepers for that. This shows a good sign of mutual trust among the shopkeepers and customers indicating that may come from the malls the small retailers will be retaining their regular customers at least giving them enough to sustain in this world.

TABLE No: 5.2.17
Price tag attached with the product

	Price tag attached with the product	Frequency	Percent	Valid Percent	Cumulative Percent
Valid	Yes	179	76.2	76.2	76.2
	No	56	23.8	23.8	100.0
	Total	235	100.0	100.0	

Source: Field Survey 2012

GRAPH No: 5.2.17
Price tag attached with the product

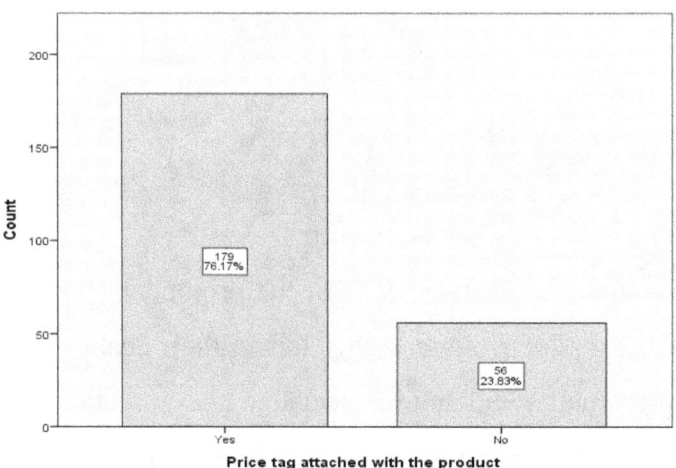

It is evident from the above table that nearly 76.17 % of the customers visiting the small retail houses have responded that they have come across a price tag attached with the product, while 23.83 % of the customers visiting the small retail houses have not seen the Price tag attached with the product.

Hence, it can be interpreted that small retail shopkeepers are attaching a price tag with most of the products and majority of the respondents also feel so.

It can thus be concluded that the shopkeepers are concerned and concentrating on making the price tag attached with the product for the satisfaction of the customers.

TABLE No: 5.2.18
Window Shopping experienced by the Respondents

	Window Shopping	Frequency	Percent	Valid Percent	Cumulative Percent
Valid	Always	66	28.1	28.1	28.1
	Sometimes	131	55.7	55.7	83.8
	Never	38	16.2	16.2	100.0
	Total	235	100.0	100.0	

Source: Field Survey 2012

GRAPH No: 5.2.18
Window Shopping experienced by the Respondents

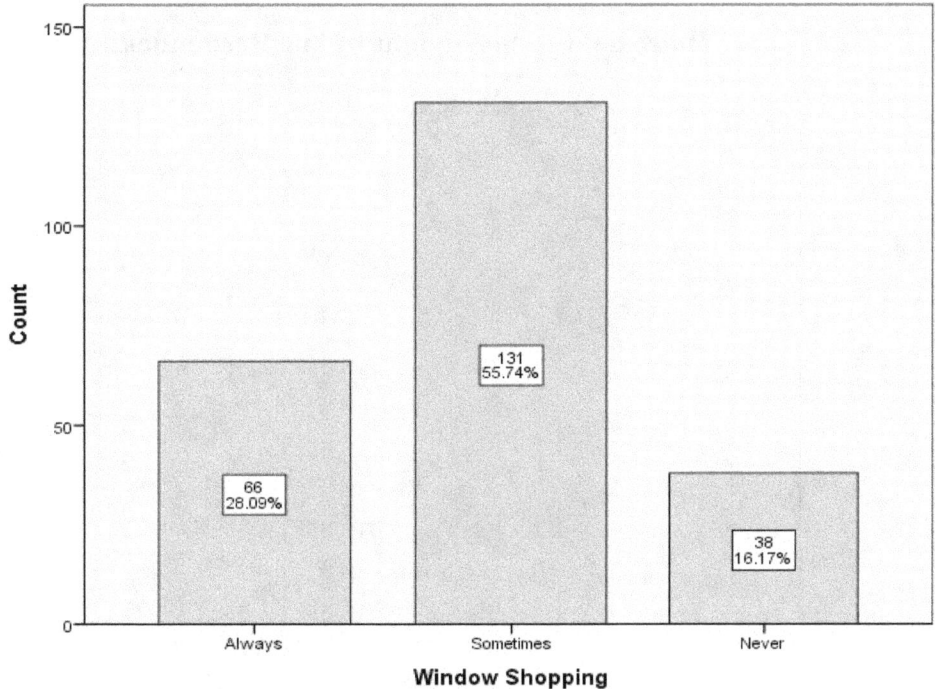

The table given above reflects that 28.09 % of the customers visiting the small retail houses always window shop at a small retail shop, 55.74 % of the respondents visiting the small retail houses sometimes do window shopping at a small retail shop while 16.17 % of the customers visiting the small retail houses never visit a small retail shop for window shopping.

It is interpreted that approximately 80 % of the respondents are many a times doing window shopping at the small retail shops.

Hence it is suggested to the small retail shopkeepers to concentrate on window dressing of the shop to increase the number of footfall in the shop.

TABLE No: 5.2.19

Household Items bought by the Respondents

Household Items		Frequency	Percent	Valid Percent	Cumulative Percent
Valid	Always	118	50.2	50.2	50.2
	Sometimes	104	44.3	44.3	94.5
	Never	13	5.5	5.5	100.0
	Total	235	100.0	100.0	

Source: Field Survey 2012

GRAPH No: 5.2.19

Household Items bought by the Respondents

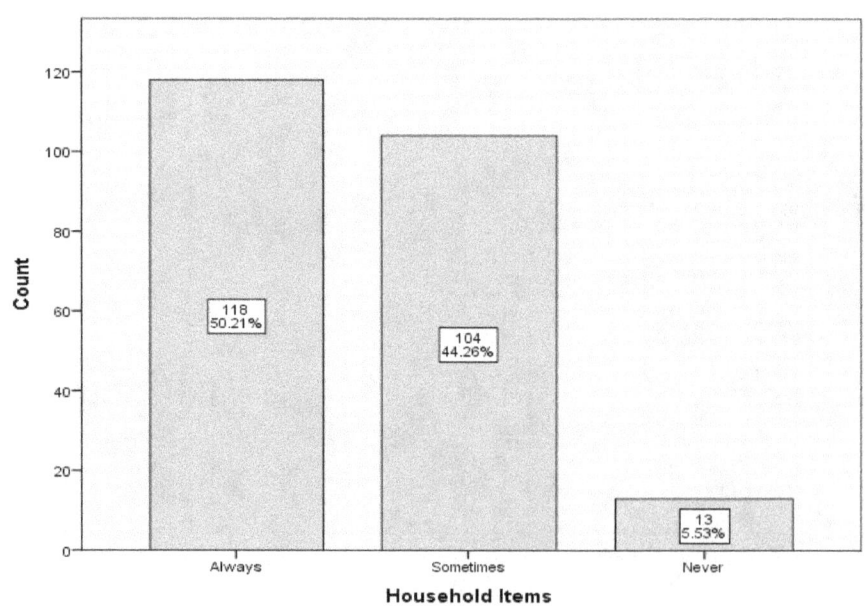

The above table shows 50.21 % of the customers visiting the small retail houses are of the opinion that they always visit the shop to buy household items, 44.26 % of these customers visiting the small retail houses only sometimes buy household items while 5.53 % of the customers visiting the small retail houses never visit the shop to buy only household items.

It can be interpreted that approximately 50 % of the respondents are always going to the small retail shops for purchase of household items while remaining 50 % are not so much interested in the household items available at the small retail shops.

Hence it can be suggested that the shopkeepers should take care that they should keep items other than household in which the customers are interested. They should keep stock of all types of items / products at their shops.

TABLE No: 5.2.20

Grocery bought by the Respondents

Grocery		Frequency	Percent	Valid Percent	Cumulative Percent
Valid	Always	161	68.5	68.5	68.5
	Sometimes	55	23.4	23.4	91.9
	Never	19	8.1	8.1	100.0
	Total	235	100.0	100.0	

Source: Field Survey 2012

GRAPH No: 5.2.20

Grocery bought by the Respondents

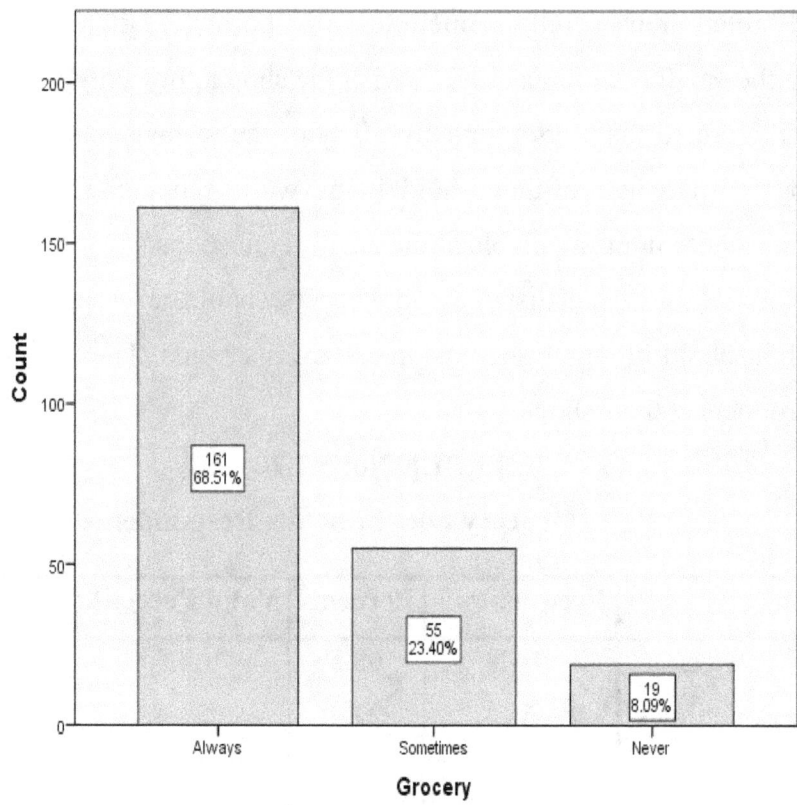

Above table reflects that 68.51% of the respondents visiting the small retail houses always visit the shop to buy grocery, 23.40 % of the respondents visiting the small retail houses visit sometimes to buy grocery or other items from the shop while only 8.09% of the respondents visiting the small retail houses never purchase grocery from the small retailers.

It can be interpreted that a large majority of the respondents visit small kirana shops for purchasing grocery hence the shopkeepers should concentrate on the quality of grocery items being bought by the customers and should also take care that they are always available whenever the customer demands for them.

TABLE No: 5.2.21
Quality of Customer Service experienced by the Respondents

Quality of Customer Service		Frequency	Percent	Valid Percent	Cumulative Percent
Valid	Highly Dissatisfied	13	5.5	5.5	5.5
	Dissatisfied	11	4.7	4.7	10.2
	Neutral	67	28.5	28.5	38.7

Satisfied	120	51.1	51.1	89.8
Highly Satisfied	24	10.2	10.2	100.0
Total	**235**	**100.0**	**100.0**	

Source: Field Survey 2012

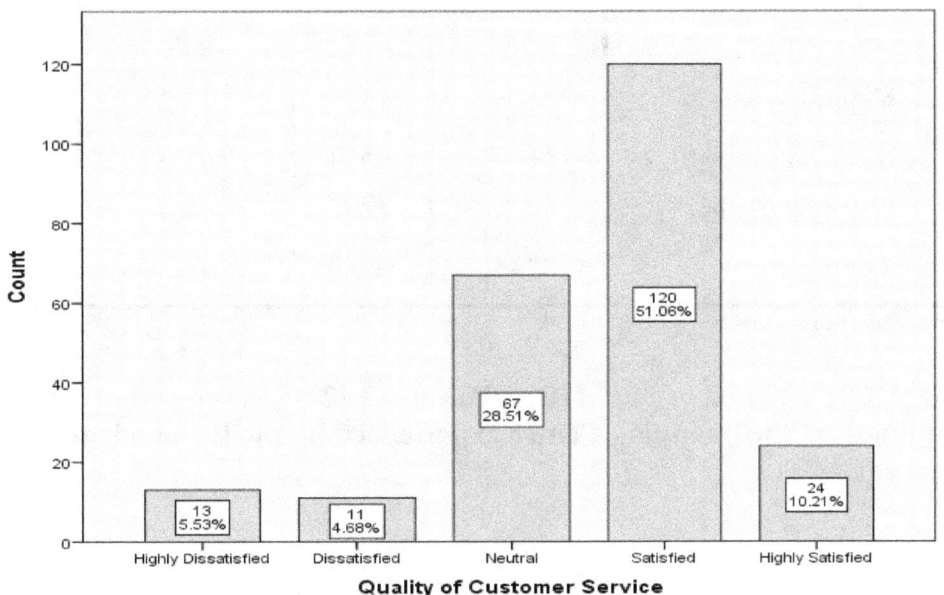

GRAPH No: 5.2.21
Quality of Customer Service experienced by the Respondents

The above graph displays that 5.53 % of the respondents visiting the small retail houses are highly dissatisfied with the quality of customer service provided by the small retailers, 4.68 % of the respondents visiting the small retail houses are dissatisfied, 28.51 % of the respondents visiting the small retail houses are neutral about it.

It is good to see that 51.06 % of the respondents visiting the small retail houses are satisfied with the quality of customer service while 10.21 % of the respondents visiting the small retail houses are highly satisfied with the services. It can be inferred that around 62 % of the respondents show a good satisfaction level regarding the quality of services provided by the small retailers. It can be concluded that the small retail shopkeepers are providing service of very good quality which satisfies the customers coming to their shop for purchase of various items like household goods, grocery etc.

It is suggested to the shopkeepers that though 62% of the respondents are satisfied with them but simultaneously it cannot be neglected that 38 % is not a small number of customers. They should understand the requirements of these customers also by talking to them or asking their expectations and try to take sincere efforts to satisfy them.

TABLE No: 5.2.22
Cleanliness of the Shopping Centre experienced by the Respondents

Cleanliness of the Shopping Centre		Frequency	Percent	Valid Percent	Cumulative Percent
Valid	Highly Dissatisfied	2	.9	.9	.9
	Dissatisfied	13	5.5	5.5	6.4
	Neutral	31	13.2	13.2	19.6
	Satisfied	154	65.5	65.5	85.1
	Highly Satisfied	35	14.9	14.9	100.0
	Total	**235**	**100.0**	**100.0**	

Source: Field Survey 2012

GRAPH No: 5.2.22
Cleanliness of the Shopping Centre experienced by the Respondents

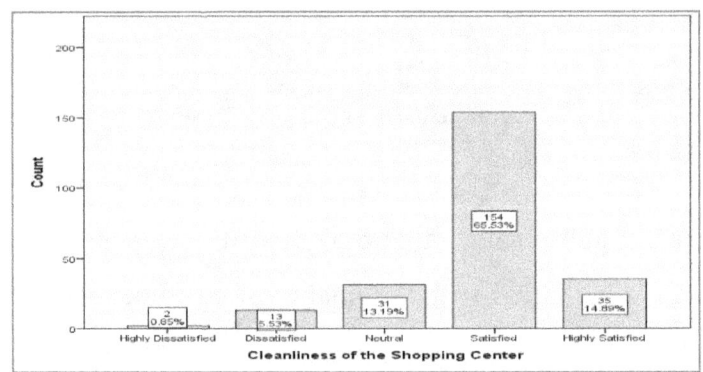

The table given above indicates that 0.85 % of the respondents visiting the small retail houses are highly dissatisfied with the cleanliness of the shopping centre, 5.53 % of the customers visiting the small retail houses are dissatisfied, 13.19 % customers visiting the small retail houses are Cleanliness of the Shopping Centre as neutral. Only 65.5 % of the customers visiting the small retail houses have rated Cleanliness of the Shopping Centre as satisfied, 14.89 % customers visiting the small retail houses are highly satisfied with the Cleanliness of the Shopping Centre.

It can be interpreted that a majority of respondents shows satisfaction with the cleanliness of the shopping centre. They feel that the shops and the surroundings are kept clean by the shopkeepers which make them satisfied remain loyal with the shop.

It can hence be concluded that Cleanliness of the Shopping Centre is an important factor for rating the shopping experience. Customers visiting the small retail houses are happy if the surroundings and all the items in the shop are kept clean.

TABLE No: 5.2.23
Security Arrangement experienced by the Respondents

Security Arrangement		Frequency	Percent	Valid Percent	Cumulative Percent
Valid	Highly Dissatisfied	11	4.7	4.7	4.7
	Dissatisfied	20	8.5	8.5	13.2
	Neutral	106	45.1	45.1	58.3
	Satisfied	73	31.1	31.1	89.4
	Highly Satisfied	25	10.6	10.6	100.0
	Total	235	100.0	100.0	

Source: Field Survey 2012

GRAPH No: 5.2.23
Security Arrangement experienced by the Respondents

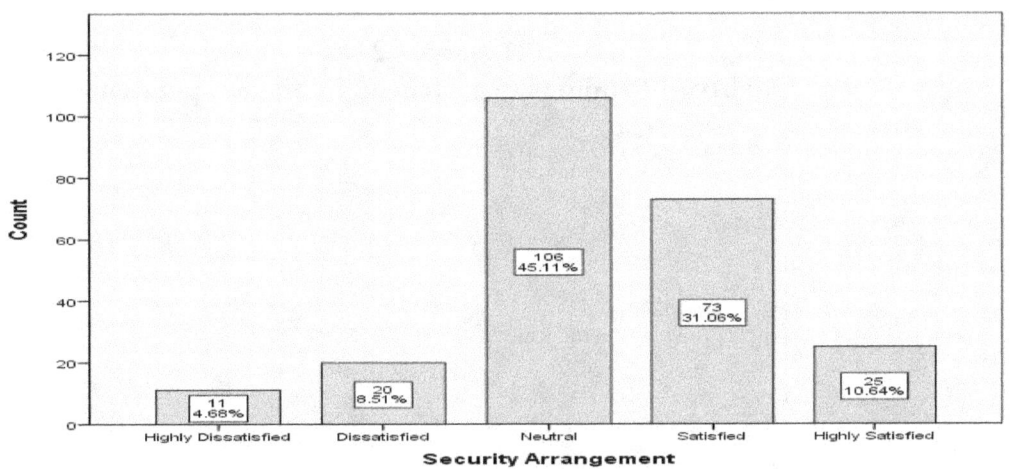

The above graph shows 45.11 % customers visiting the small retail houses are neutral with regard to Security arrangement, while 31 % of the customers visiting the small retail houses are satisfied with the Security Arrangement of the shop. 10.64 % of customers visiting the small retail houses are highly satisfied and 8.51 % of the customers visiting the small retail houses are dissatisfied. It can also be seen that only 4.68 % customers visiting the small retail houses are highly dissatisfied with the security arrangements of the shop.

It can be interpreted that only approximately 40% of the respondents are satisfied with the security arrangements of the small retail shops. But the tables given before had shown that a large majority of customers are satisfied with their shopping experience at the small retail shops.

Hence it can be concluded that Security Arrangement is not a very important criterion for choosing a shop.

TABLE No: 5.2.24
Quality of Products experienced by the Respondents

Quality of Products		Frequency	Percent	Valid Percent	Cumulative Percent
Valid	Highly Dissatisfied	1	.4	.4	.4
	Dissatisfied	9	3.8	3.8	4.3
	Neutral	40	17.0	17.0	21.3
	Satisfied	138	58.7	58.7	80.0
	Highly Satisfied	47	20.0	20.0	100.0
	Total	235	100.0	100.0	

Source: Field Survey 2012

GRAPH No: 5.2.24
Quality of Products experienced by the Respondents

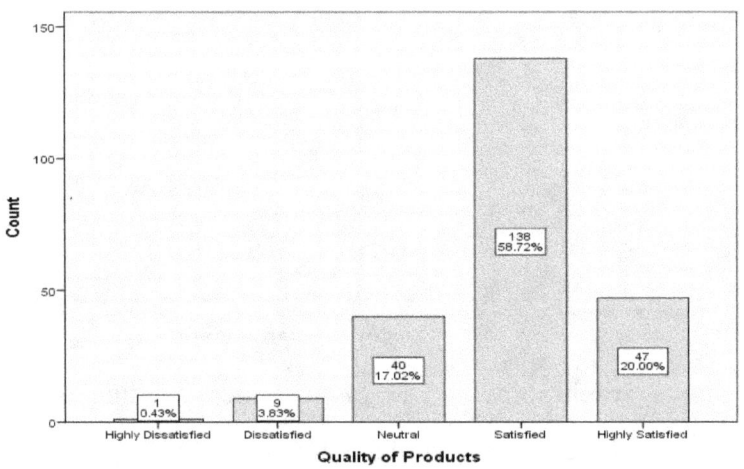

Above graph shows that majority i.e. nearly 58 % of the customers visiting the small retail houses are satisfied with the quality of the products, followed by 20% of the customers visiting the small retail houses responding as highly satisfied and 17.02 % customers visiting the small retail houses responding as neutral towards the quality of products. Only 3.83% and 0.43% of the customers visiting the small retail houses are dissatisfied and highly dissatisfied with the quality of the products.

It can be interpreted that majority of respondents are satisfied with the quality of products available. It is a good sign for the small retailers as quality of products is a very important factor considered by the customers while denoting their shopping experience.

It is suggested to the shopkeepers to retain the quality of products and to make it more better by keeping more variety of brands to attract customers to their shops.

It can be concluded that the small retailers are taking lot of efforts to maintain and upgrade the quality of products available at their shops. They have to compete with the large retailers for sustaining in this competition hence sincere efforts are required. The brands known to the customers and required by the customers should be always available. The grocery items should be clean and hygienically kept with product price tags on them.

TABLE No: 5.2.25
Ease in Purchase experienced by the Respondents

	Ease in Purchase	Frequency	Percent	Valid Percent	Cumulative Percent
Valid	Highly Dissatisfied	5	2.1	2.1	2.1
	Dissatisfied	21	8.9	8.9	11.1
	Neutral	53	22.6	22.6	33.6
	Satisfied	115	48.9	48.9	82.6
	Highly Satisfied	41	17.4	17.4	100.0
	Total	**235**	**100.0**	**100.0**	

Source: Field Survey 2012

GRAPH No: 5.2.25
Ease in Purchase experienced by the Respondents

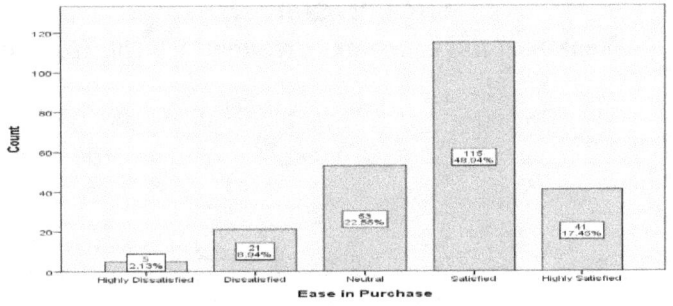

The above graph reflects that 8.94 % of the customers visiting the small retail houses and 2.13 % of the customers visiting the small retail houses are dissatisfied and highly dissatisfied with the ease of purchase factor in their shopping experience, 48.94 % of the customers visiting the small retail houses are satisfied with the ease of purchase, 22.55 % of the customers visiting the small retail houses are neutral towards ease of purchase while 17.45 % of the customers visiting the small retail houses are highly satisfied with this factor while rating their shopping experience.

It can be interpreted that around 65 % of the respondents feel it is easy to purchase from the small retail houses. While remaining 35 % of the respondents do not feel so. Ease of purchase is a very important factor in the shopping experience of the respondents.

It is suggested to the small retail shoppers that though 65 % respondents are satisfied with the ease of purchase still 35 % of the respondents who are not satisfied is not a small percentage, they have to concentrate on this lot of customers more importantly. They can take measures such as preparing brochures containing product and their prices available at their counter using which they can place their order. Taking delivery orders on phone can be a good choice.

TABLE No: 5.2.26
Nearness to House experienced by the Respondents

	Nearness to House	Frequency	Percent	Valid Percent	Cumulative Percent
Valid	Highly Dissatisfied	7	3.0	3.0	3.0
	Dissatisfied	41	17.4	17.4	20.4
	Neutral	61	26.0	26.0	46.4
	Satisfied	89	37.9	37.9	84.3
	Highly Satisfied	37	15.7	15.7	100.0
	Total	235	100.0	100.0	

Source: Field Survey 2012

GRAPH No: 5.2.26
Nearness to House experienced by the Respondents

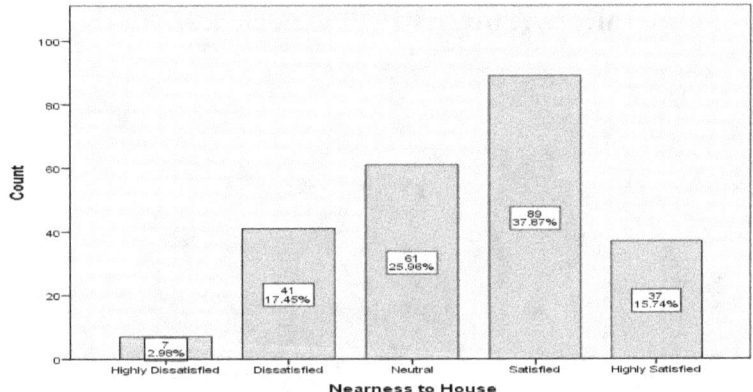

The above graph shows 37.87 % of the customers visiting the small retail houses are satisfied with the shop being near to their house and 15.74 % of the respondents visiting the small retail houses are highly satisfied with the same. It can also be noted that 25 % of the customers visiting the small retail houses are neutral towards this factor 17.45 % of the customers are dissatisfied and 2.98 % of the customers visiting the small retail houses are highly dissatisfied with the shop being near to their house.

Hence it can be interpreted that majority of the customers are satisfied with the fact that the shops are near to their house.

It can be concluded that the nearness of the shops to the houses is an important factor contributing to the satisfaction of the respondents and that they are more concentrating on buying their grocery from nearby store rather than travelling far away from their house.

TABLE No: 5.2.27
Comparatively Lower Prices experienced by the Respondents

Comparatively Lower Prices		Frequency	Percent	Valid Percent	Cumulative Percent
Valid	Highly Dissatisfied	6	2.6	2.6	2.6
	Dissatisfied	20	8.5	8.5	11.1
	Neutral	83	35.3	35.3	46.4
	Satisfied	98	41.7	41.7	88.1
	Highly Satisfied	28	11.9	11.9	100.0
	Total	**235**	**100.0**	**100.0**	

Source: Field Survey 2012

GRAPH No: 5.2.27

Comparatively Lower Prices experienced by the Respondents

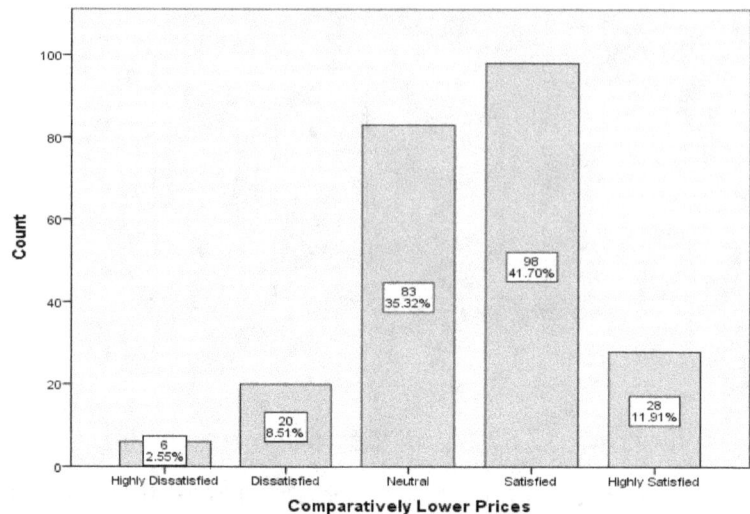

The table given above reflects that 11.91 % of the respondents visiting the small retail houses are highly satisfied and 41.70 % of the respondents visiting the small retail houses are satisfied with the lower prices of the products in the shops they visit as compared to the other shops in the nearby vicinity, while 35 % visiting the small retail houses of the customers are neutral about it. It can also see that 11.91 % of the customers visiting the small retail houses are dissatisfied with the Prices at the shop they purchase from as compared to the other shops while 2.55 % of the customers visiting the small retail houses are highly dissatisfied. It can be interpreted that only approximately 50% of the customers show their satisfaction towards the prices of the products being comparatively lower than the near by shops in the vicinity. It can hence be concluded that the shopkeepers are not paying attention towards comparing the prices of the products at their shops with the nearby shops. This may affect the retention of customers with them. It is suggested to the shopkeepers that their prices should be at par with those at other nearby shops or lower as Price is the major factor considered for selecting a shop for shopping grocery.

TABLE No: 5.2.28
Emotionality in Buying Motive experienced by the Respondents

Emotionality in Buying Motive	Frequency	Percent	Valid Percent	Cumulative Percent
Valid Highly Dissatisfied	6	2.6	2.6	2.6

Dissatisfied	29	12.3	12.3	14.9
Neutral	84	35.7	35.7	50.6
Satisfied	90	38.3	38.3	88.9
Highly Satisfied	26	11.1	11.1	100.0
Total	**235**	**100.0**	**100.0**	

Source: Field Survey 2012

GRAPH No: 5.2.28
Emotionality in Buying Motive experienced by the Respondents

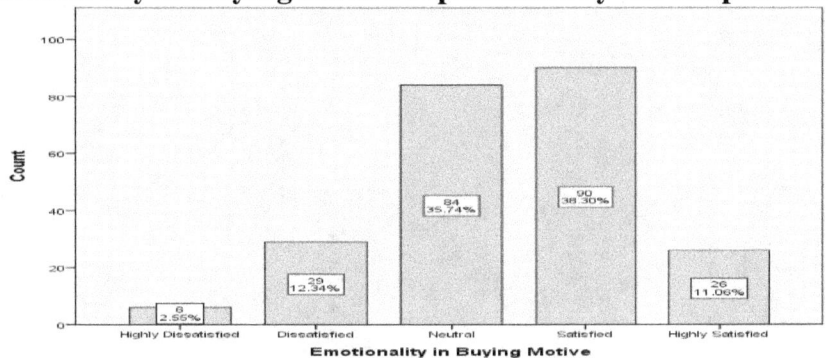

Above graph shows 38.3 % customers visiting the small retail houses are satisfied with the emotionality in buying followed by 35.74 % of the respondents visiting the small retail houses who are neutral about this factor. 11.06 % of the customers visiting the small retail houses are highly satisfied with the emotionality in buying behavior. We can also observe that 12.34 % of the customers visiting the small retail houses are dissatisfied and 2.55 % of the customers visiting the small retail houses are highly dissatisfied with this factor.

It can thus be construed that less than 50 % of the respondents are satisfied with the emotionality aspect in the buying motive. This shows that the respondents are not purchasing on the emotional terms. It can thus be concluded that the respondents are not feeling emotionally attached to the shopkeepers and this may result in their not being loyal to them.

It is suggested that should build a good rapport with the respondents as emotionality in buying behaviour is an important factor while selecting a shop.

TABLE No: 5.2.29
Level of Lighting experienced by the Respondents

Level of Lighting		Frequency	Percent	Valid Percent	Cumulative Percent
Valid	Highly Dissatisfied	1	.4	.4	.4
	Dissatisfied	22	9.4	9.4	9.8

Neutral	77	32.8	32.8	42.6
Satisfied	103	43.8	43.8	86.4
Highly Satisfied	32	13.6	13.6	100.0
Total	**235**	**100.0**	**100.0**	

Source: Field Survey 2012

GRAPH No: 5.2.29
Level of Lighting experienced by the Respondents

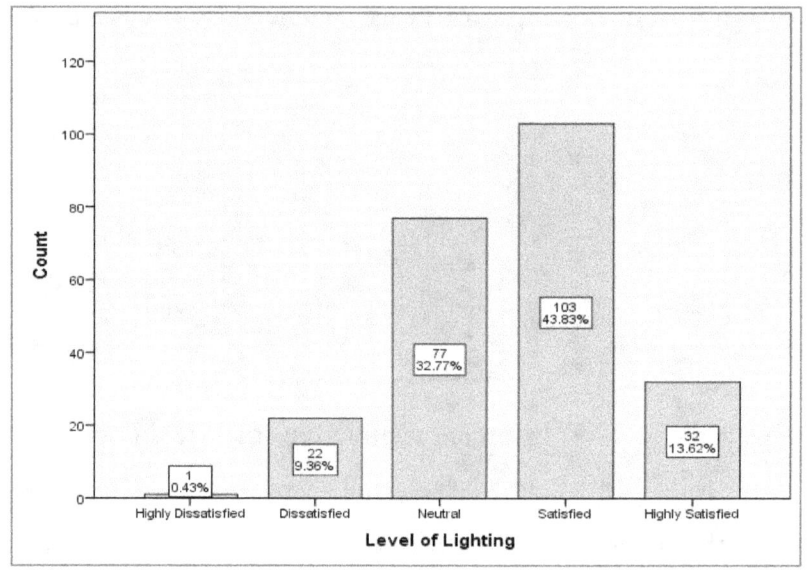

The above graph indicates that 43.83 % of the customers visiting the small retail houses are satisfied with the Level of Lighting of the shop while 32.77 % customers visiting the small retail houses are neutral towards this factor. 13.62 % of the customers visiting the small retail houses are highly satisfied with the level of lighting. Only 9.36 % of the customers visiting the small retail houses are dissatisfied with the level of lighting.

It can be interpreted that around 47 % of the respondents are satisfied with the lighting level of the shops while 53 % of the respondents are not satisfied.

It can be concluded that a majority of respondents feel that the lighting level of the shops is not optimum and thus causes obstruction in their buying process.

Hence it is suggested to the shopkeepers that Level of Lighting is an important factor while rating the shopping experience of the customers and hence they should take care that lighting at their shops is at the optimum level of visibility and helps in making the purchase more convenient.

TABLE No: 5.2.30
Crowd Level experienced by the Respondents

Crowd Level		Frequency	Percent	Valid Percent	Cumulative Percent
Valid	Highly Dissatisfied	3	1.3	1.3	1.3
	Dissatisfied	42	17.9	17.9	19.1
	Neutral	90	38.3	38.3	57.4
	Satisfied	79	33.6	33.6	91.1
	Highly Satisfied	21	8.9	8.9	100.0
	Total	235	100.0	100.0	

Source: Field Survey 2012

GRAPH No: 5.2.30
Crowd Level experienced by the Respondents

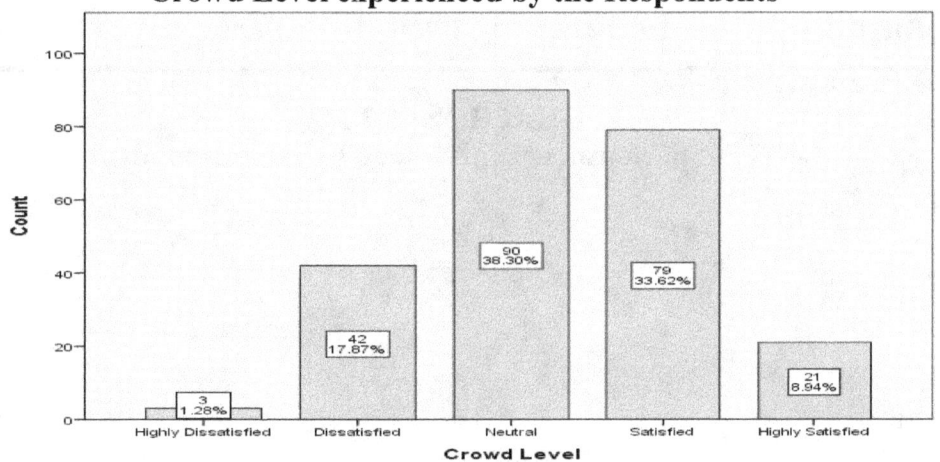

Above table depicts that 38.30 % customers visiting the small retail houses are neutral towards the level of crowd at the shops, while 33.62 % of the customers visiting the small retail houses are satisfied by the. It can also be seen that 8.94 % of the customers visiting the small retail houses are highly satisfied with this factor. 17.87 % of the crowd level customers visiting the small retail houses are dissatisfied with the crowd level while shopping and only 1.28 % of the customers visiting the small retail houses are highly dissatisfied with this crowd level.

Hence it can be interpreted that only 40 % of the respondents are satisfied with the crowd level at the small retail houses from where they do their purchase and remaining 60 % of the respondents feel that the shops are crowded and thus they are not satisfied. Hence we can say that crowd is also rated as an important factor for shopping experience by the customer.

It is thus suggested to the shopkeepers that they should take care that the customers are not feeling inconvenient because of the level of crowd at their shops. They can think of taking a helping hand during the rush hours.

TABLE No: 5.2.31
Level of Spaciousness experienced by the Respondents

	Level of Spaciousness	Frequency	Percent	Valid Percent	Cumulative Percent
Valid	Highly Dissatisfied	10	4.3	4.3	4.3
	Dissatisfied	34	14.5	14.5	18.7
	Neutral	68	28.9	28.9	47.7
	Satisfied	92	39.1	39.1	86.8
	Highly Satisfied	31	13.2	13.2	100.0
	Total	**235**	**100.0**	**100.0**	

Source: Field Survey 2012

GRAPH No: 5.2.31
Level of Spaciousness experienced by the Respondents

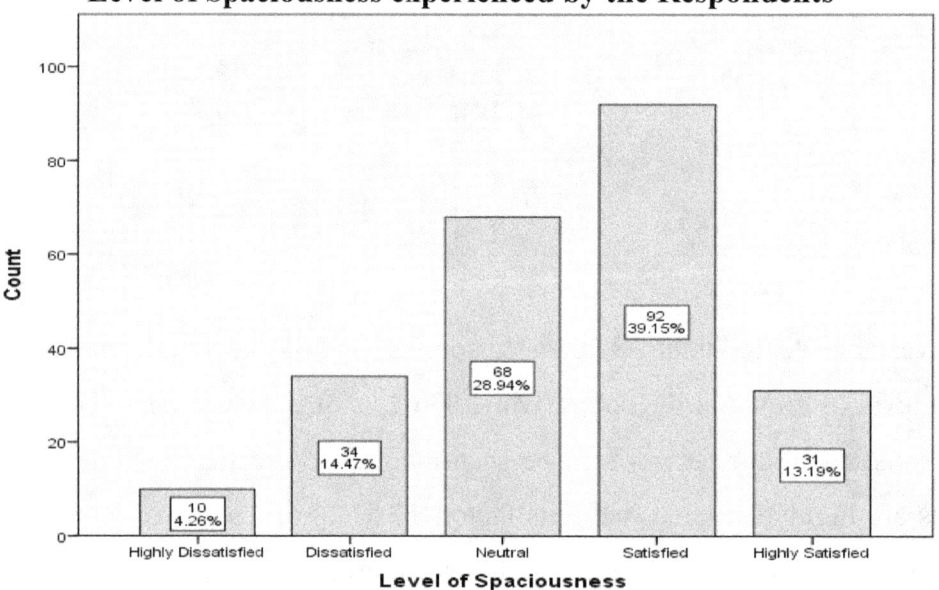

Above graph shows that 39.15 % of the customers visiting the small retail houses are satisfied with the level of spaciousness followed by 28.94 % of the customers visiting the small retail houses are neutral towards this factor while rating the shopping experience. 13.19 % customers visiting the small retail houses are highly satisfied with the level of spaciousness of the shop. There are 14.47 % customers visiting the small retail houses who are dissatisfied with the level of spaciousness of the shop and also 4.26 % customers visiting the small retail houses highly dissatisfied with the level of spaciousness of the shop.

It can be interpreted that around 52 % of the respondents are satisfied with the level of space available at the small retail houses while the remaining 47 % of the respondents do not feel so. It is suggested to the shopkeepers that they should arrange the goods at their shops in such a way that the empty space in the shop gets increased and the respondents find it easier to reach to the products and feel comfortable with the space available.

Hence it can be concluded that customers consider Level of Spaciousness as one of the important factor while rating the shopping experience.

TABLE No: 5.2.32
Mode of Payment experienced by the Respondents

Mode of Payment		Frequency	Percent	Valid Percent	Cumulative Percent
Valid	Highly Dissatisfied	13	5.5	5.5	5.5
	Dissatisfied	15	6.4	6.4	11.9
	Neutral	37	15.7	15.7	27.7
	Satisfied	141	60.0	60.0	87.7
	Highly Satisfied	29	12.3	12.3	100.0
	Total	**235**	**100.0**	**100.0**	

Source: Field Survey 2012

GRAPH No: 5.2.32
Mode of Payment experienced by the Respondents

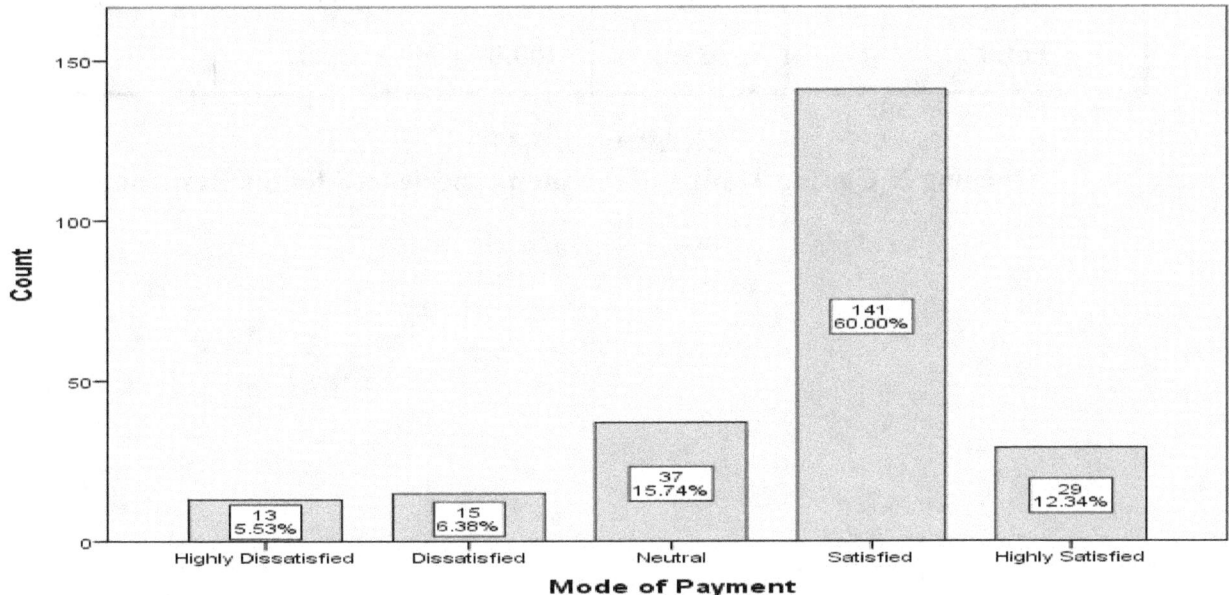

The table given above indicates that 5.53 % of the customers visiting the small retail houses are highly dissatisfied with the mode of payment and 6.38 % of the customers visiting the small retail houses are dissatisfied with the same. We can see that 60 % of the customers visiting the small retail houses are satisfied with the mode of payment implemented by the small retail shop owners. Also we can see that 15.74 % customers visiting the small retail houses visiting the small retail houses are neutral about the mode of payment, while 12.34 % customers visiting the small retail houses are highly satisfied with the mode of payment of the shop.

It can thus be interpreted that majority of the customers are satisfied with the mode of payment at the small retail houses. It can be concluded that the mode of payment is one of the important factor to be considered while rating the shopping experience as it decides the satisfaction level of the customers.

TABLE No: 5.2.33
Opening & Closing Timing of the shop experienced by the Respondents

Opening & Closing Timing		Frequency	Percent	Valid Percent	Cumulative Percent
Valid	Highly Dissatisfied	9	3.8	3.8	3.8
	Dissatisfied	17	7.2	7.2	11.1
	Neutral	27	11.5	11.5	22.6
	Satisfied	121	51.5	51.5	74.0
	Highly Satisfied	61	26.0	26.0	100.0
	Total	**235**	**100.0**	**100.0**	

Source: Field Survey 2012

GRAPH No: 5.2.33
Opening & Closing Timing of the shop experienced by the Respondents

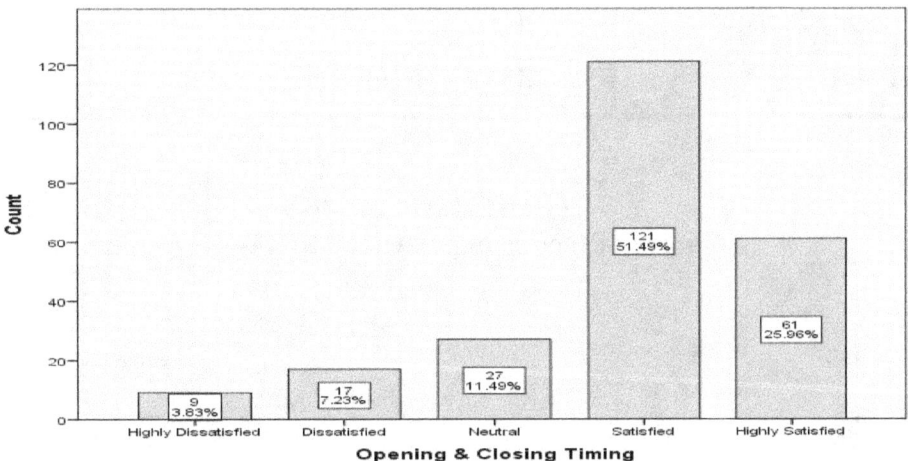

The graph given above shows that 3.83% of the customers visiting the small retail houses are highly dissatisfied with the Opening & Closing Timing of the shop, 7.23 % of the customers visiting the small retail houses are dissatisfied with the Opening & Closing Timings, and 11.49% of the customers visiting the small retail houses are neutral about the Opening & Closing Timing of the shop. 51.49 % of the customers visiting the small retail houses are satisfied with the Opening & Closing Timing of the shop. While 25.96 % of the customers visiting the small retail houses are highly satisfied with this factor. It can be inferred that around 77 % of the respondents visiting the small retail houses of Kolhapur city are satisfied with the opening and closing timings of the shops. It is suggested to the shopkeepers that they should maintain the same timings and can also give a thought on increasing it if feasible. To attract the unsatisfied respondents they can even think of the option of providing their contact number to the customers to call them up in case they require some product in emergency and to make it available also.

We can conclude that Opening & Closing Timing of the shop matters a lot while rating the shopping experience.

TABLE No: 5.2.34
Choice of Goods experienced by the Respondents

	Choice of Goods	Frequency	Percent	Valid Percent	Cumulative Percent
Valid	Highly Dissatisfied	3	1.3	1.3	1.3
	Dissatisfied	7	3.0	3.0	4.3
	Neutral	50	21.3	21.3	25.5
	Satisfied	145	61.7	61.7	87.2

Highly Satisfied	30	12.8	12.8	100.0
Total	**235**	**100.0**	**100.0**	

Source: Field Survey 2012

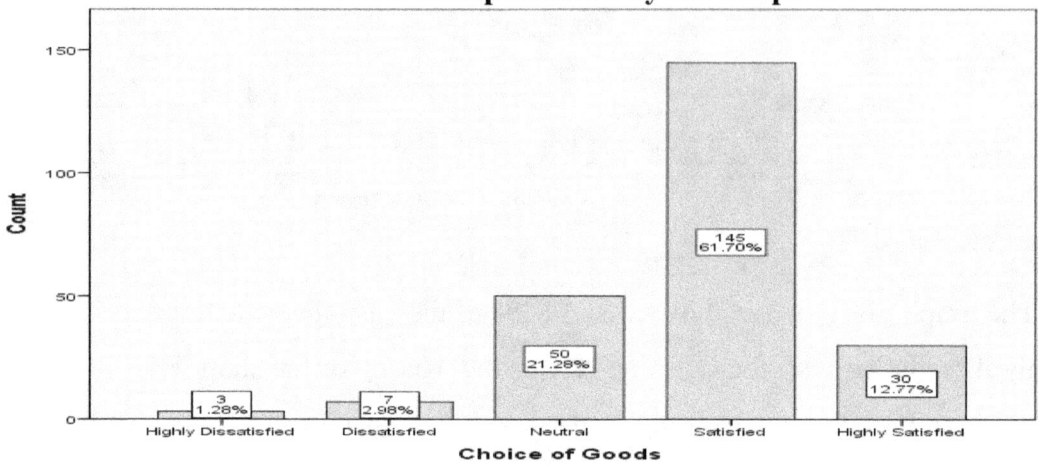

GRAPH No: 5.2.34
Choice of Goods experienced by the Respondents

The above graph reflects that 1.28 % of the customers visiting the small retail houses and 2.98 % of the customers visiting the small retail houses are highly dissatisfied and dissatisfied with the choice of goods stacked in the shop. 21.28 % of the customers visiting the small retail houses are neutral about this criterion. While, 61.70 % of the customers visiting the small retail houses are satisfied with the choice of goods stacked in the shop. Also 12.77 % of the customers visiting the small retail houses are highly satisfied with the factor choice of goods during their shopping experience. It can thus be construed that around 73 % of the respondents are satisfied with the choice of goods available at the small retail shops while 27 % of them are dissatisfied.

It can be concluded that the shopkeepers are paying attention towards making the choice available in the selection of goods. Here we can say that customers are quite happy about the choice of goods stacked by the shopkeeper.

TABLE No: 5.2.35
Reputation of the Shop experienced by the Respondents

	Reputation of the Shop	Frequency	Percent	Valid Percent	Cumulative Percent
Valid	Highly Dissatisfied	3	1.3	1.3	1.3
	Dissatisfied	14	6.0	6.0	7.2
	Neutral	61	26.0	26.0	33.2

Satisfied	116	49.4	49.4	82.6
Highly Satisfied	41	17.4	17.4	100.0
Total	**235**	**100.0**	**100.0**	

Source: Field Survey 2012

GRAPH No: 5.2.35
Reputation of the Shop experienced by the Respondents

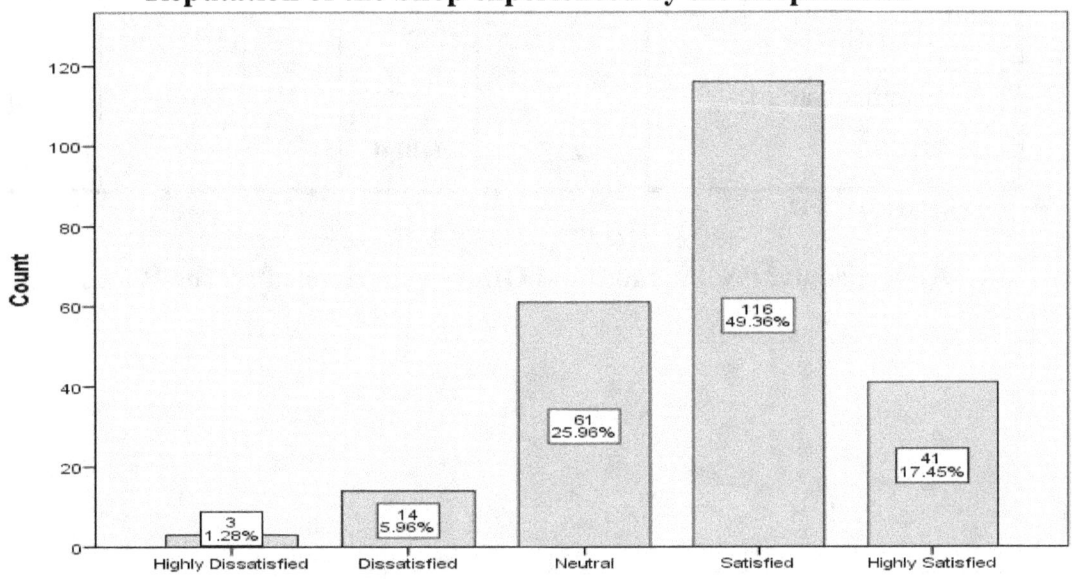

The above graph shows 1.28 % of customers visiting the small retail houses and 5.96 % of customers visiting the small retail houses are highly dissatisfied and dissatisfied with the reputation of the shop during the shopping experience. Here, we also see that 25.96 % of the customers visiting the small retail houses are neutral towards this factor. 49.36 % of customers visiting the small retail houses are satisfied with the Reputation of the Shop. While 17.45 % of the customers visiting the small retail houses are highly satisfied with the Reputation of the Shop. It can be interpreted that 66 % of the customers visiting the small retail houses are satisfied with the reputation of the shop while 34 % of the customers are not satisfied.

It is suggested to the shopkeepers that they should concentrate on improving the reputation of the shop. They can take measures such as improving the environment at and around the shop.

TABLE No: 5.2.36
Advertisement & Promotional Offers experienced by the Respondents

Advertisement & Promotional Offers		Frequency	Percent	Valid Percent	Cumulative Percent
Valid	Highly Dissatisfied	6	2.6	2.6	2.6
	Dissatisfied	29	12.3	12.3	14.9
	Neutral	45	19.1	19.1	34.0
	Satisfied	123	52.3	52.3	86.4
	Highly Satisfied	32	13.6	13.6	100.0
	Total	**235**	**100.0**	**100.0**	

Source: Field Survey 2012

GRAPH No: 5.2.36
Advertisement & Promotional Offers experienced by the Respondents

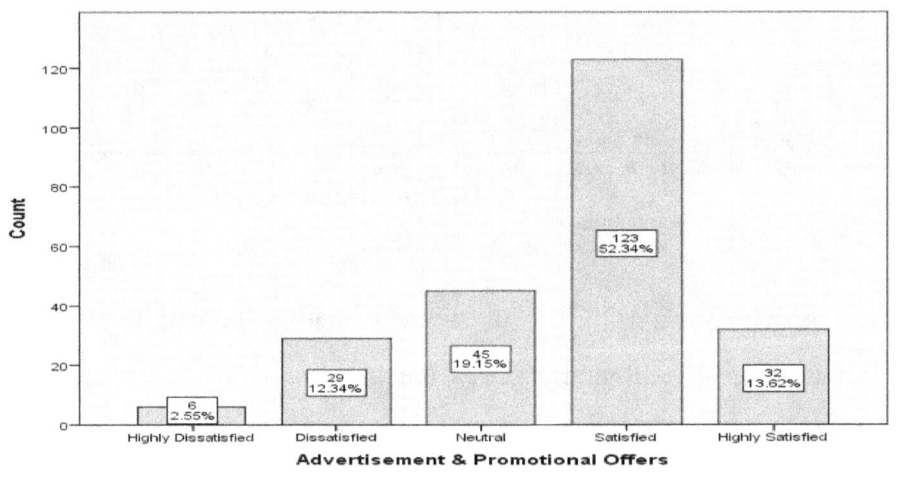

Above graph shows 2.55 % customers visiting the small retail houses are highly dissatisfied and 12.34 % customers visiting the small retail houses are dissatisfied with the Advertisement & Promotional Offers implemented by the shopkeepers. 19.15 % of the customers visiting the small retail houses are neutral about this factor during their shopping experience and 52.34 % of the customers visiting the small retail houses are satisfied with the Advertisement & Promotional Offer supplemented by the shopkeepers.

It can be interpreted that a majority of the customers i.e. around 66 % are satisfied with the advertisement and promotional offers by the small retail shops.

It is suggested to the shopkeepers that they can think of providing attractive promotional offers and schemes in consultation with the respective company. Here we can say that customers do pay attention on the Advertisement & Promotional Offers given by the company.

TABLE No: 5.2.37
Credit Facility experienced by the Respondents

Credit Facility		Frequency	Percent	Valid Percent	Cumulative Percent
Valid	Highly Dissatisfied	12	5.1	5.1	5.1
	Dissatisfied	40	17.0	17.0	22.1
	Neutral	55	23.4	23.4	45.5
	Satisfied	92	39.1	39.1	84.7
	Highly Satisfied	36	15.3	15.3	100.0
	Total	**235**	**100.0**	**100.0**	

Source: Field Survey 2012

GRAPH No: 5.2.37
Credit Facility experienced by the Respondents

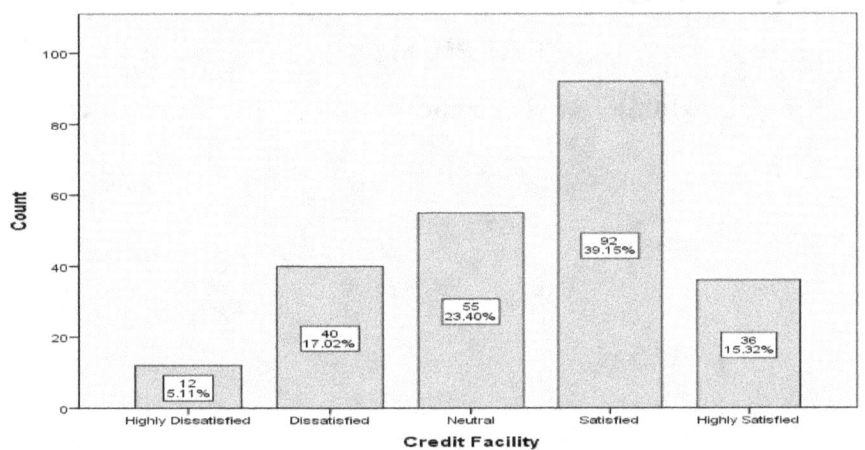

The above graph depicts that 5.11 % of customers visiting the small retail houses are highly dissatisfied and 17.02 % of the customers visiting the small retail houses are dissatisfied with the credit facility given by the shop. While 23.4 % of the customers visiting the small retail houses are neutral about the Credit Facility offered by the shop. 39.15 % of the customers visiting the small retail houses are satisfied with the Credit Facility offered by the shop. We can also see that 15.32 % of the customers visiting the small retail houses are highly satisfied with this offer. It can thus be inferred that around 54 % of the customers are satisfied with credit facility while 46 % of them are not satisfied. We know that in business the policy of most of the shopkeepers is that of "NO

CREDIT". But when it comes to small kirana shops of Kolhapur city we find that the customers generally look for as per need shopping and monthly billing. It is suggested to the shopkeepers that they should try to find out which customers are actually in need of credit facility and then try to satisfy them so as to retain them. Here we can say that Credit Facility offered by the shop is an important factor while deciding about the shop.

TABLE No: 5.2.38
Home Delivery experienced by the Respondents

Home Delivery		Frequency	Percent	Valid Percent	Cumulative Percent
Valid	Highly Dissatisfied	26	11.1	11.1	11.1
	Dissatisfied	41	17.4	17.4	28.5
	Neutral	49	20.9	20.9	49.4
	Satisfied	90	38.3	38.3	87.7
	Highly Satisfied	29	12.3	12.3	100.0
	Total	**235**	**100.0**	**100.0**	

Source: Field Survey 2012

GRAPH No: 5.2.38

Home Delivery experienced by the Respondents

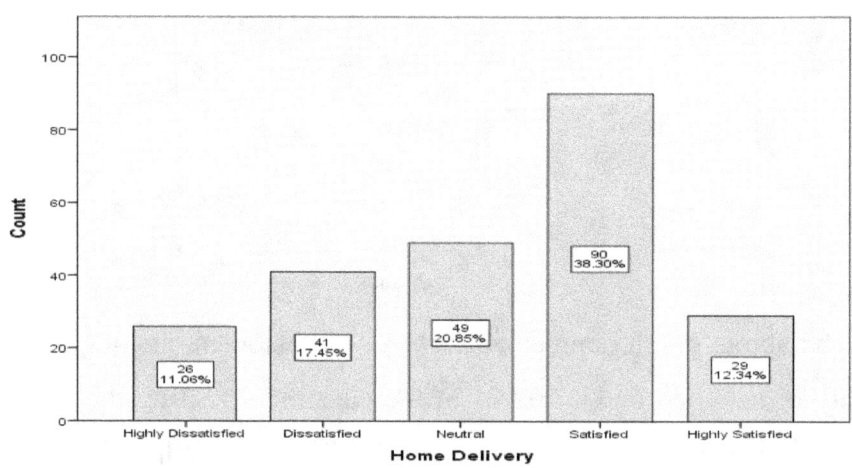

The table given above shows that 11.06 % of the customers visiting the small retail houses are highly dissatisfied and 17.45 % of customers visiting the small retail houses are dissatisfied with the home delivery services provided by the small retailers. It can also be seen that 20 % of the customers visiting the small retail houses were neutral about the Home Delivery service offered by the shop and 38.30 % of the customers visiting the small retail houses are satisfied with Home Delivery service offered by the shop. We can also see that 12.34 % of the customers visiting the small retail houses are highly satisfied with the home delivery facility of the shop. It can be interpreted that only 50 % of the respondents visiting the small retail houses are satisfied with the home delivery services provided by the small retailers which means that the shopkeepers have to go a long way to satisfy the remaining 50 % of the customers visiting the small retail houses. It can be suggested to the small retailers that they should offer home delivery services effectively on time. They can think of charging a meagre amount for the home delivery services provided if the house of the respondent is at a greater distance. Delivery at nearby houses should be made free. Here Home Delivery service is considered to be very important factor while rating the shopping experience.

TABLE No: 5.2.39
Display of Goods experienced by the Respondents

Display of Goods		Frequency	Percent	Valid Percent	Cumulative Percent
Valid	Highly Dissatisfied	15	6.4	6.4	6.4
	Dissatisfied	8	3.4	3.4	9.8
	Neutral	57	24.3	24.3	34.0
	Satisfied	125	53.2	53.2	87.2
	Highly Satisfied	30	12.8	12.8	100.0
	Total	235	100.0	100.0	

Source: Field Survey 2012

GRAPH No: 5.2.39
Display of Goods experienced by the Respondents

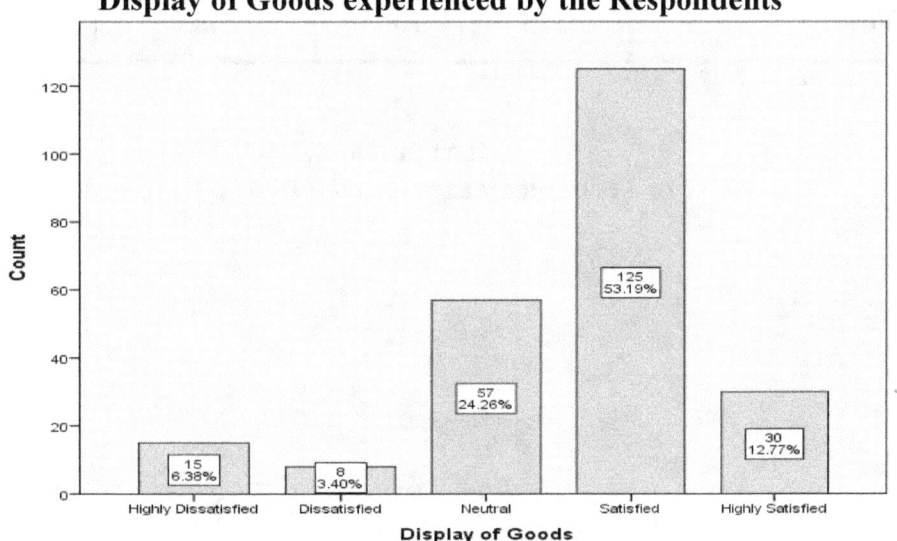

Above graph indicates that 6.38 % of the customers visiting the small retail houses and 3.40 % of customers visiting the small retail houses are highly dissatisfied and dissatisfied respectively with the display of goods in the shop. 24.26 % of the customers visiting the small retail houses are neutral about Display of Goods and 53.19 % of the customers visiting the small retail houses are satisfied with the Display of Goods while 12.77 % of the customers visiting the small retail houses are highly satisfied with the Display of Goods. It can be deduced that 65 % of the respondents visiting the small retail houses are satisfied with the display of goods done at the shop by the shopkeepers. It can also be seen that 35% of the respondents reflect dissatisfaction with the display. It can be suggested to the shopkeepers that they should make the display more attractive to improve the visibility of the goods. This will help the customers to know whether the goods desired by them are available or not. It will also help the shopkeepers as a good display results in impulsive buying many a times.

TABLE No: 5.2.40

Use of Technology experienced by the Respondents

	Use of Technology	Frequency	Percent	Valid Percent	Cumulative Percent
Valid	Highly Dissatisfied	18	7.7	7.7	7.7
	Dissatisfied	32	13.6	13.6	21.3
	Neutral	58	24.7	24.7	46.0
	Satisfied	91	38.7	38.7	84.7
	Highly Satisfied	36	15.3	15.3	100.0
	Total	**235**	**100.0**	**100.0**	

Source: Field Survey 2012

GRAPH No: 5.2.40

Use of Technology experienced by the Respondents

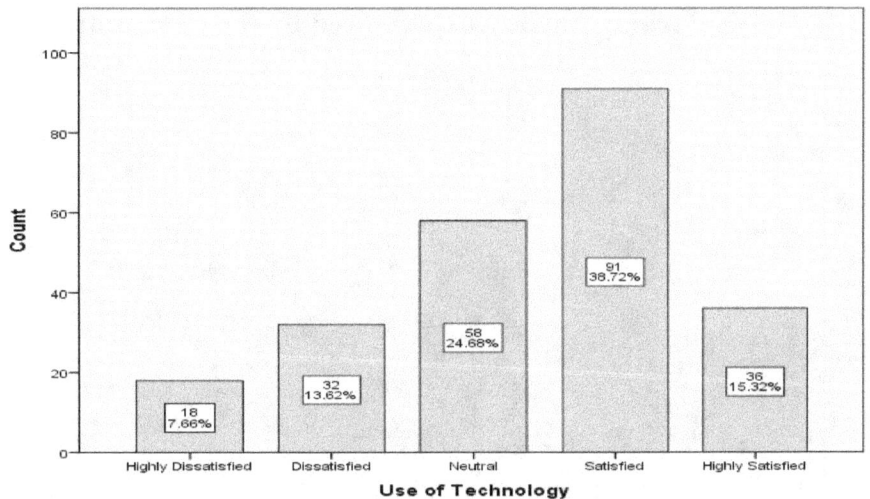

The graph given above shows that 7.66 % of the customers visiting the small retail houses and 13.62 % of the customers visiting the small retail houses are highly dissatisfied and dissatisfied respectively with the use of technology at the small retail shops. 24.68 % of the customers visiting the small retail houses are neutral towards this factor. 38.72 % of the customers visiting the small retail houses are satisfied with the Use of Technology followed by 15.32 % of the customers visiting the small retail houses are highly satisfied with this factor of use of technology. It can be interpreted that more than 55 % of the respondents visiting the small retail houses are satisfied with the use of technology. It is suggested to the small retailers that they should try to use technology in their daily procedure like taking orders on phone, computerised billing etc. This will make the process more transparent and satisfying for the respondents.

TABLE No: 5.2.41

Parking Facility experienced by the Respondents

	Parking Facility	Frequency	Percent	Valid Percent	Cumulative Percent
Valid	Highly Dissatisfied	6	2.6	2.6	2.6
	Dissatisfied	38	16.2	16.2	18.7
	Neutral	40	17.0	17.0	35.7
	Satisfied	107	45.5	45.5	81.3
	Highly Satisfied	44	18.7	18.7	100.0
	Total	**235**	**100.0**	**100.0**	

Source: Field Survey 2012

GRAPH No: 5.2.41

Parking Facility experienced by the Respondents

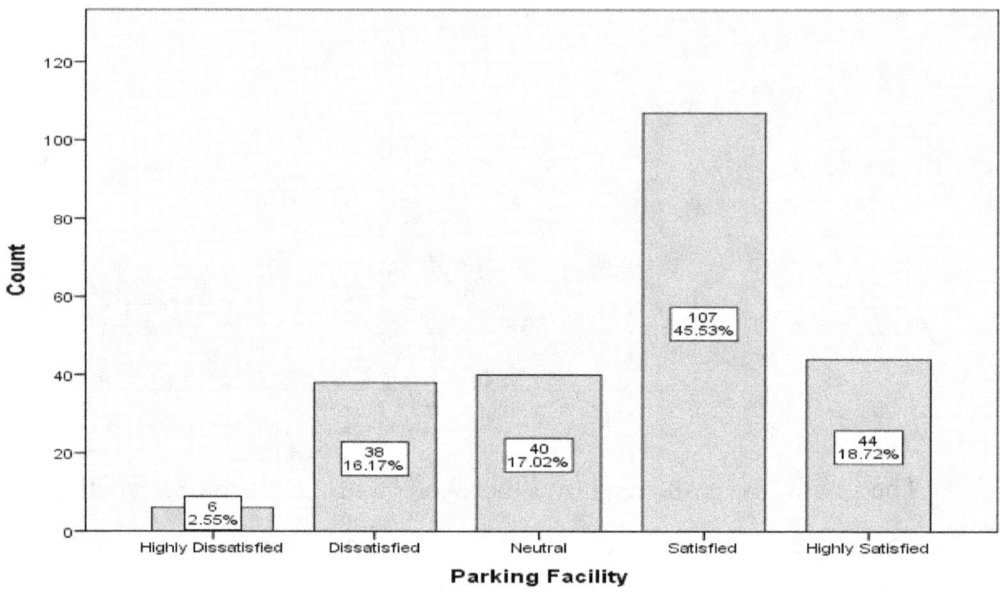

Above graph shows 2.55 % of the customers visiting the small retail houses are highly dissatisfied and 16.17 % of the customers visiting the small retail houses are dissatisfied with the parking facility factor at the shopping experience. 17 % customers visiting the small retail houses are neutral about the parking facility While, 45.53 % of the customers visiting the small retail houses are satisfied with the parking facility of the shop, and 18 % customers visiting the small retail houses are highly satisfied. It can be interpreted that around 63 % of the respondents visiting the small retail houses are satisfied with the parking facility available at the small retail shops. It can thus be concluded that parking facility is not a major point of concern for the respondents doing purchase from small retail houses as majority of them are satisfied with it.

TABLE No: 5.2.42
Quality of Customer Service experienced by the Respondents

Quality of Customer Service		Frequency	Percent	Valid Percent	Cumulative Percent
Valid	Not at all Important	5	2.1	2.1	2.1
	Of little Importance	20	8.5	8.5	10.6
	Moderate Importance	32	13.6	13.6	24.3
	Important	111	47.2	47.2	71.5
	Extremely Important	67	28.5	28.5	100.0
	Total	**235**	**100.0**	**100.0**	

Source: Field Survey 2012

GRAPH No: 5.2.42
Quality of Customer Service experienced by the Respondents

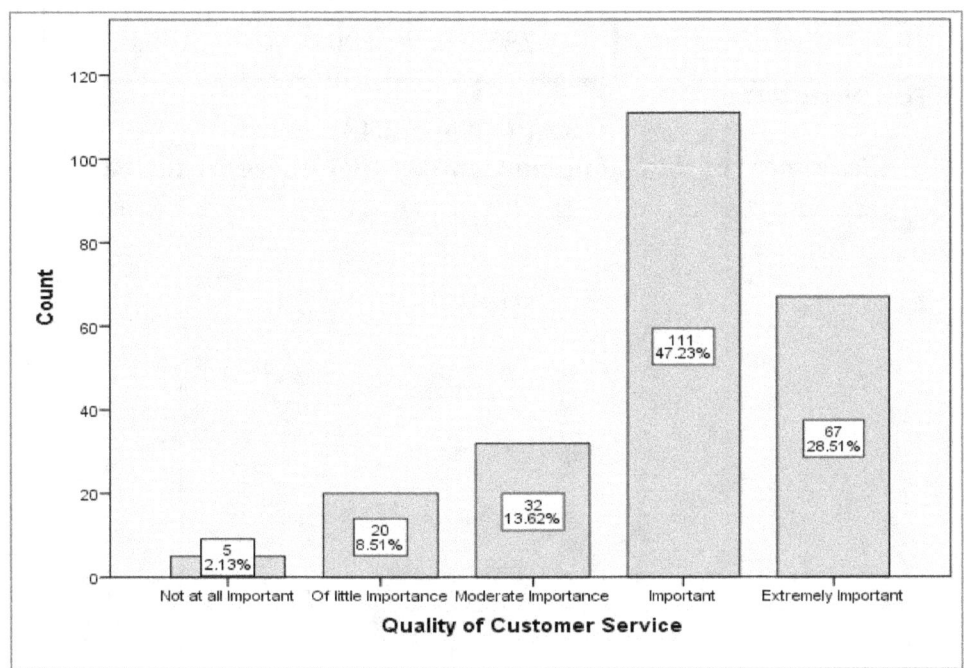

Above graph indicates that 2.13 % of the customers visiting the small retail houses grade quality of customer service as not at all important, 8.51 % of the respondents visiting the small retail houses say it is of little importance, 13.62 % of the customers visiting the small retail houses rate it as moderate importance, 47.23 % of the customers visiting the small retail houses grade Quality of Customer Service as important and 28.51 % of the customers visiting the small retail houses grade this factor as extremely important. It can be inferred that 75 % of the respondents visiting the small retail houses feel that quality of customer service is an important factor in deciding the retail shop for purchase. Hence, quality of customer service is an important factor to be concentrated by the small retail shop owners.

TABLE No: 5.2.43
Cleanliness of the Shopping Centre experienced by the Respondents

Cleanliness of the Shopping Centre	Frequency	Percent	Valid Percent	Cumulative Percent
Valid Not at all Important	2	.9	.9	.9

	Of little Importance	13	5.5	5.5	6.4
	Moderate Importance	34	14.5	14.5	20.9
	Important	121	51.5	51.5	72.3
	Extremely Important	65	27.7	27.7	100.0
	Total	**235**	**100.0**	**100.0**	

Source: Field Survey 2012

GRAPH No: 5.2.43
Cleanliness of the Shopping Centre experienced by the Respondents

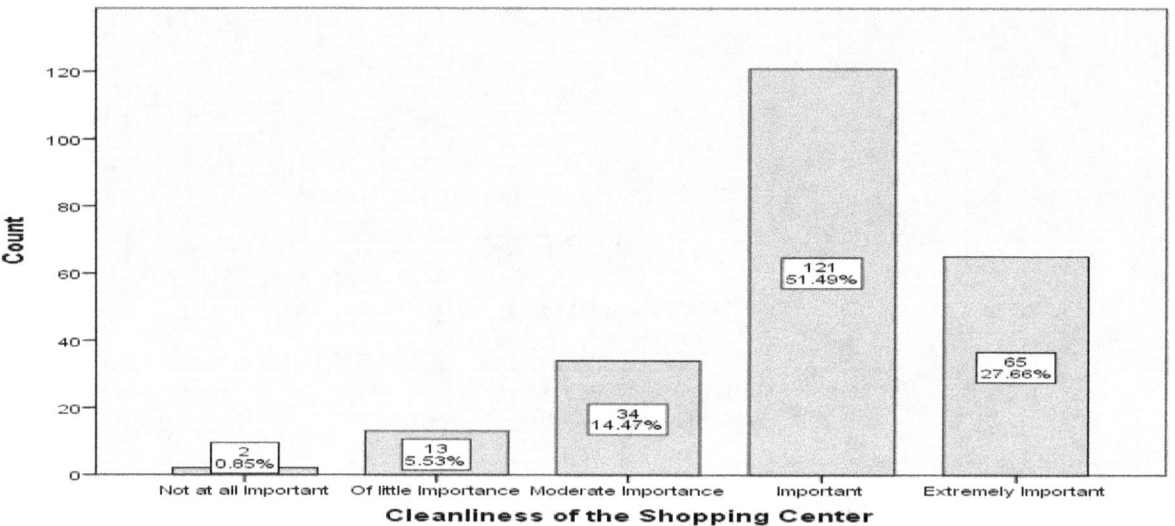

Above graph clearly states that 51.49 % customers visiting the small retail houses have graded Cleanliness of the Shopping Centre as an important factor while 27.66 % of the customers visiting the small retail houses have graded it as extremely important. It can also be seen that 14.47 % of the respondents visiting the small retail houses give it moderate importance, 5.53 % customers visiting the small retail houses say it is of little importance and 0.85 % customers visiting the small retail houses say it is not at all important. It can be interpreted that around 77 % of the respondents visiting the small retail houses grade cleanliness of the shopping centre as an important factor in the choice of the retail house. Thus it can be concluded that Cleanliness of the Shopping Centre is a vital part of the retailer to attract the customers.

TABLE No: 5.2.44
Security Arrangements experienced by the Respondents

Security Arrangements	Frequency	Percent	Valid Percent	Cumulative Percent
Valid Not at all Important	9	3.8	3.8	3.8

Of little Importance	33	14.0	14.0	17.9
Moderate Importance	49	20.9	20.9	38.7
Important	97	41.3	41.3	80.0
Extremely Important	47	20.0	20.0	100.0
Total	**235**	**100.0**	**100.0**	

Source: Field Survey 2012

GRAPH No: 5.2.44
Security Arrangements experienced by the Respondents

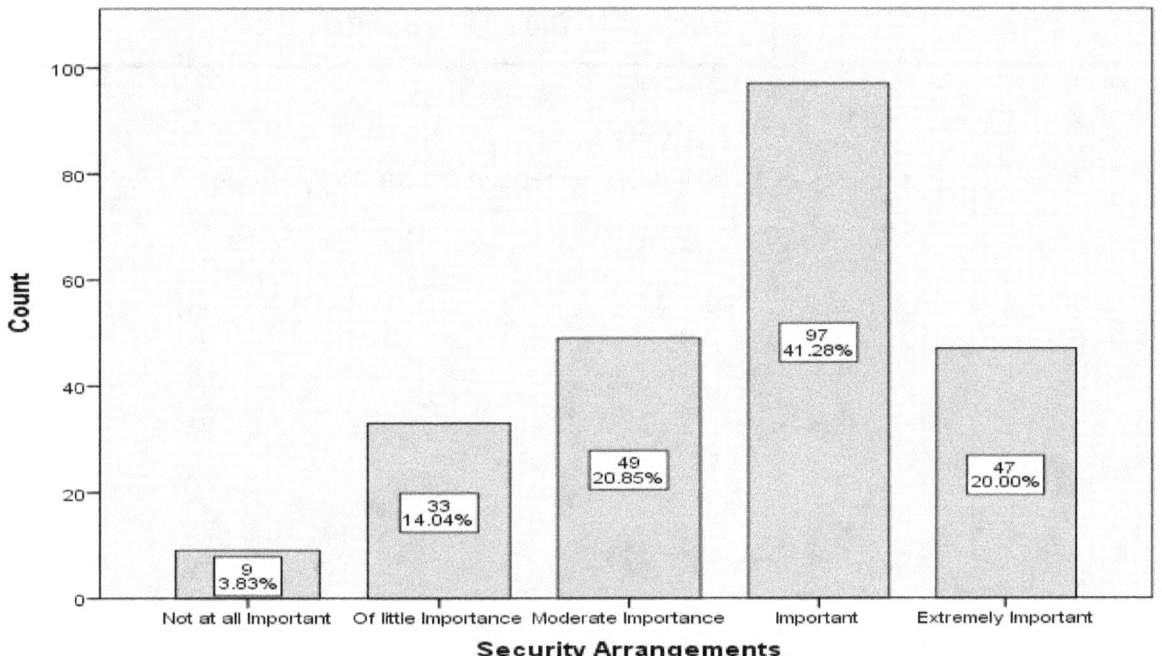

Above graph states that 41.28 % customers visiting the small retail houses have graded important to security arrangements of the Shopping Centre while 20.85 % of the customers visiting the small retail houses say security arrangements of the Shopping Centre is of moderate importance and 20 % customers visiting the small retail houses have graded security arrangements of the Shopping Centre as extremely important. It can also be observed that 14.05 % of the customers visiting the small retail houses say security arrangements of the Shopping Centre is of little importance and 3.83 % of the customers visiting the small retail houses say security arrangements of the Shopping Centre is not at all important. It can be interpreted that around 60 % of the respondents visiting the small retail houses emphasize that security arrangements at the shops is an important attribute as per the level of importance it holds in the minds of the customers.

TABLE No: 5.2.45
Quality of Products experienced by the Respondents

Quality of Products		Frequency	Percent	Valid Percent	Cumulative Percent
Valid	Not at all Important	3	1.3	1.3	1.3
	Of little Importance	4	1.7	1.7	3.0
	Moderate Importance	33	14.0	14.0	17.0
	Important	111	47.2	47.2	64.3
	Extremely Important	84	35.7	35.7	100.0
	Total	235	100.0	100.0	

Source: Field Survey 2012

GRAPH No: 5.2.45
Quality of Products experienced by the Respondents

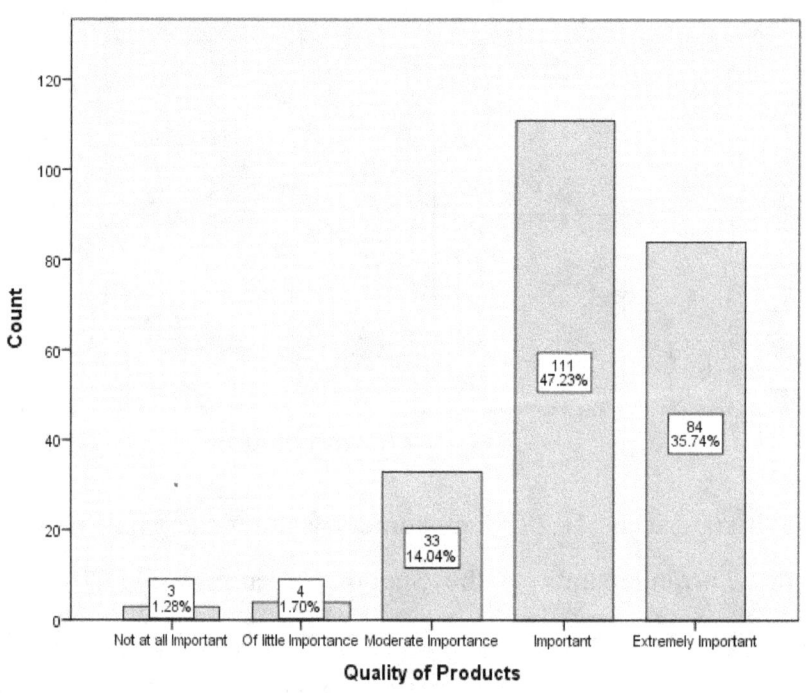

The above graph shows that 47.23 % customers have graded quality of products at the Shopping Centre while 35.74 % of the customers have graded it as extremely important. 14.04 % of the respondents say that it is of moderate importance, 1.70 % say it is of little importance while 1.28 % of the respondents say it is not at all important. It can be interpreted that around 80 % of the respondents give importance to the quality of the products available at the small retail shops in deciding the point of purchase. Hence it is suggested to the retailers that the quality of products is very important in the mind of respondents and if they do not get quality products then they may switch off to a different retail outlet. Here we can see that quality of products is a very important factor that holds the level of importance in the minds of the customer.

TABLE No: 5.2.46
Ease in Purchase experienced by the Respondents

Ease in Purchase		Frequency	Percent	Valid Percent	Cumulative Percent
Valid	Not at all Important	2	.9	.9	.9
	Of little Importance	20	8.5	8.5	9.4
	Moderate Importance	40	17.0	17.0	26.4
	Important	126	53.6	53.6	80.0
	Extremely Important	47	20.0	20.0	100.0
	Total	235	100.0	100.0	

Source: Field Survey 2012

GRAPH No: 5.2.46

Ease in Purchase experienced by the Respondents

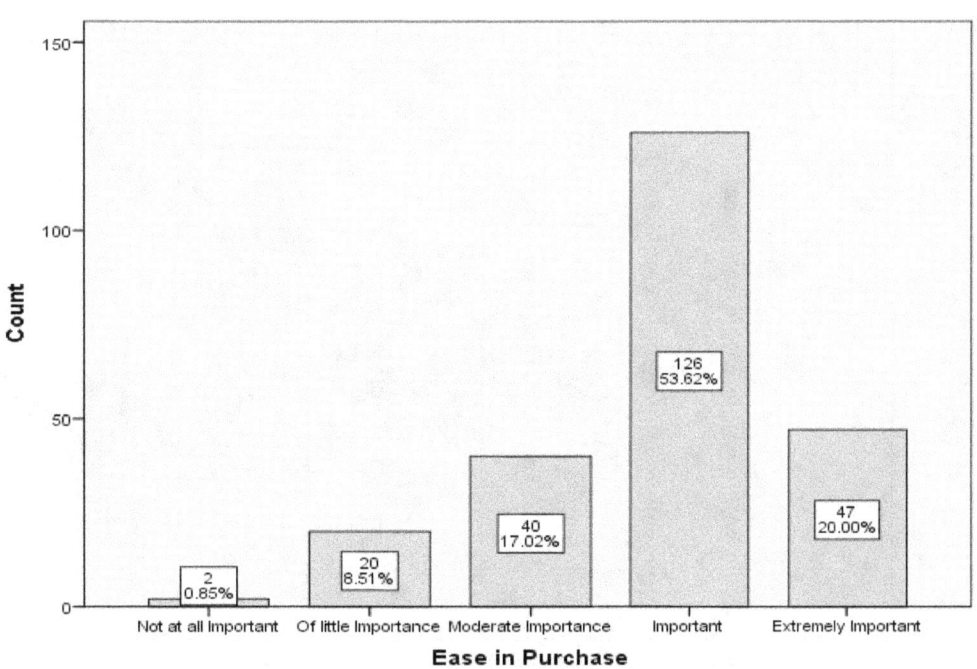

The graph given above indicates that 20 % customers feel ease in purchase as a very important factor, 53.62 % feel ease of purchase at the Shopping Centre as important. At the same time it is reflected that 17.02 % feel ease of purchase as moderately important, 8.51 % say it is of little importance while 0.85 % feel it is not at all important.

It can be deduced that 73 % of the customers feel that ease in purchase as an important factor in taking decision regarding the choice of shop.

TABLE No: 5.2.47

Nearness to House experienced by the Respondents

Nearness to House		Frequency	Percent	Valid Percent	Cumulative Percent
Valid	Not at all Important	5	2.1	2.1	2.1
	Of little Importance	36	15.3	15.3	17.4
	Moderate Importance	50	21.3	21.3	38.7
	Important	91	38.7	38.7	77.4
	Extremely Important	53	22.6	22.6	100.0
	Total	235	100.0	100.0	

Source: Field Survey 2012

GRAPH No: 5.2.47

Nearness to House experienced by the Respondents

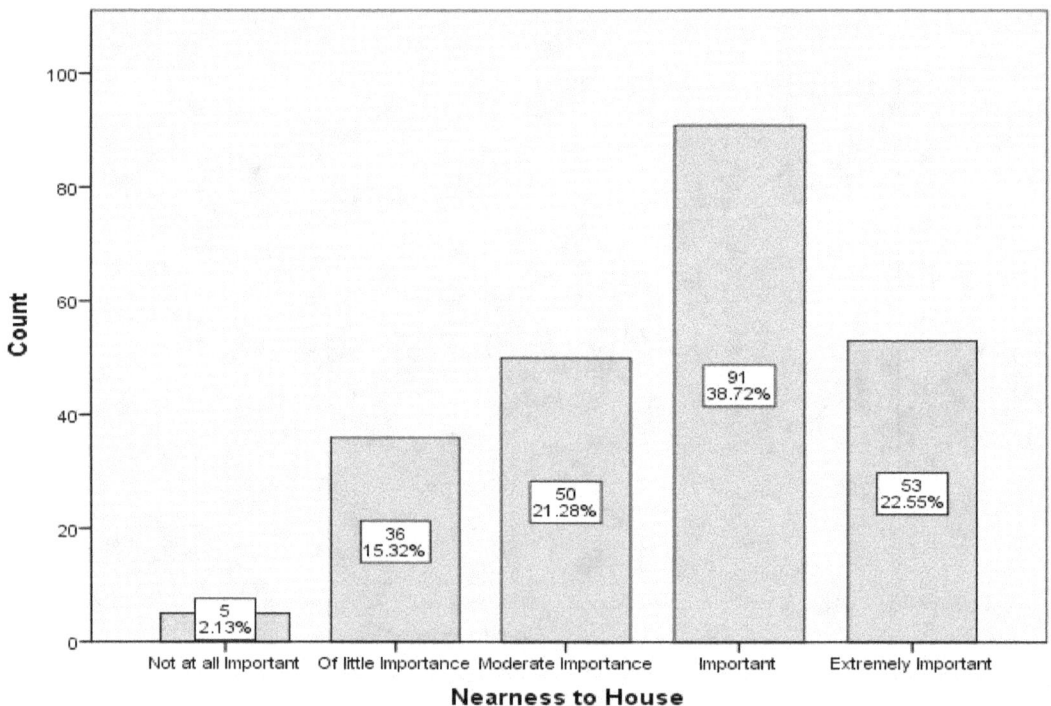

The graph given above depicts that 38.7 % customers have graded the nearness of the shop to house as an important attribute of the Shopping centre while 22.6 % of the customers have graded as extremely important and 21.3 % have graded as moderate importance. 15.32 % of the respondents say it is of little importance and 2.13 % of them say it is not all important. It can be interpreted that around 60 % of the respondents feel that the nearness to the house is an important factor thus Small retail shop or kirana shops in Kolhapur city are mostly preferred due to their nearness to house attribute.

TABLE No: 5.2.48

Comparatively Lower Prices experienced by the Respondents

Comparatively Lower Prices		Frequency	Percent	Valid Percent	Cumulative Percent
Valid	Not at all Important	2	.9	.9	.9
	Of little Importance	29	12.3	12.3	13.2
	Moderate Importance	59	25.1	25.1	38.3
	Important	84	35.7	35.7	74.0
	Extremely Important	61	26.0	26.0	100.0
	Total	235	100.0	100.0	

Source: Field Survey 2012

GRAPH No: 5.2.48

Comparatively Lower Prices experienced by the Respondents

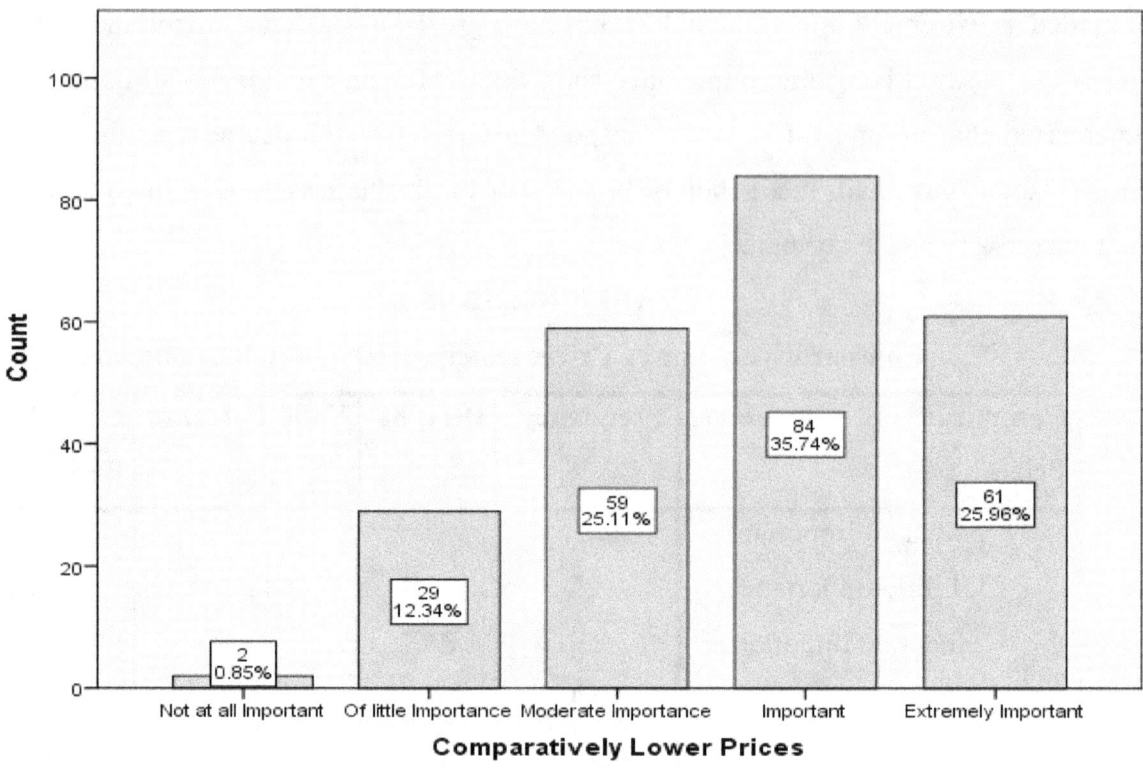

Above graph shows that 0.85 % of customers are considering the factor of comparatively Lower prices as not at all important, while 12.34 % of the customers think this factor is of little importance. 25.11 % of the customers have graded as moderate importance and 35.74 % customers have graded important to comparatively Lower prices attribute of the Shopping Centre while 25.96 % of the customers have graded as extremely important. It can thus be construed that around 60 % of the respondents find comparatively lower prices as important attribute. It can hence be concluded that out of four P's the P of price is still a very dominating attribute while considering the level of importance it holds to the Customers.

TABLE No: 5.2.49
Emotionality in Buying Motive experienced by the Respondents

	Emotionality in Buying Motive	Frequency	Percent	Valid Percent	Cumulative Percent
Valid	Not at all Important	26	11.1	11.1	11.1
	Of little Importance	36	15.3	15.3	26.4
	Moderate Importance	72	30.6	30.6	57.0
	Important	87	37.0	37.0	94.0
	Extremely Important	14	6.0	6.0	100.0

| | Total | 235 | 100.0 | 100.0 | |

Source: Field Survey 2012

GRAPH No: 5.2.49
Emotionality in Buying Motive experienced by the Respondents

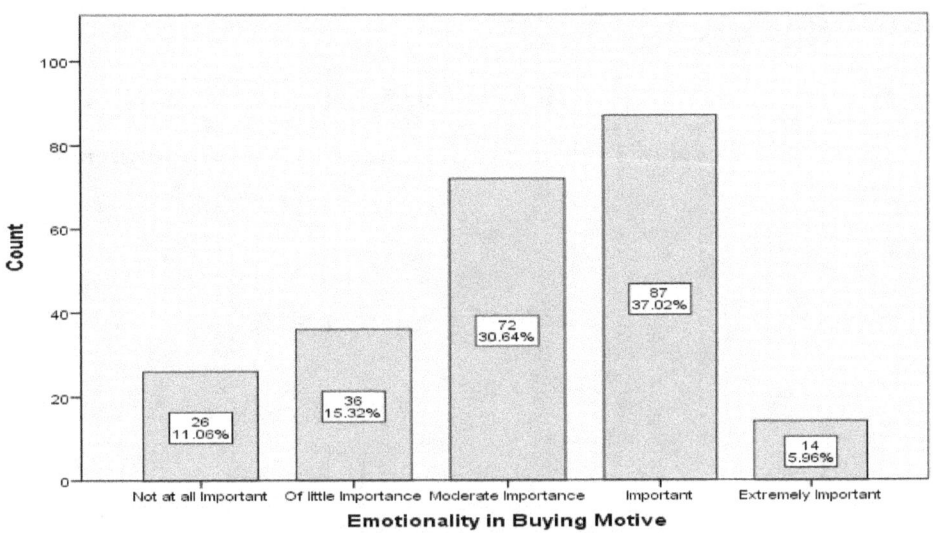

The above graph indicates that 11.06 % of the customers have graded Emotionality in buying motive as not at all important and 15.32 % customers are of the opinion that this factor is of little importance. 30.64 % of the customers have graded this attribute as moderate important and 37.02 % customers have graded important to Emotionality in buying motive of the Shopping Centre while only 5.96 % of the customers have graded Emotionality in buying motive as moderate important. It can thus be interpreted that around 42 % of the respondents say that emotionality in buying motive is important for them while remaining 58 % of the respondents do not feel so. It is a general notion that the small kirana shops in Kolhapur city are running successfully because of the emotionality in the purchase behaviour but the results here show that emotionality is not of much importance to the buyers. Here we can say that the trust or emotions attached with the shop are not considered important or of moderate importance by the customers.

TABLE No: 5.2.50
Level of Lighting experienced by the Respondents

	Level of Lighting	Frequency	Percent	Valid Percent	Cumulative Percent
Valid	Not at all Important	9	3.8	3.8	3.8
	Of little Importance	35	14.9	14.9	18.7

Moderate Importance	55	23.4	23.4	42.1
Important	99	42.1	42.1	84.3
Extremely Important	37	15.7	15.7	100.0
Total	**235**	**100.0**	**100.0**	

Source: Field Survey 2012

GRAPH No: 5.2.50

Level of Lighting experienced by the Respondents

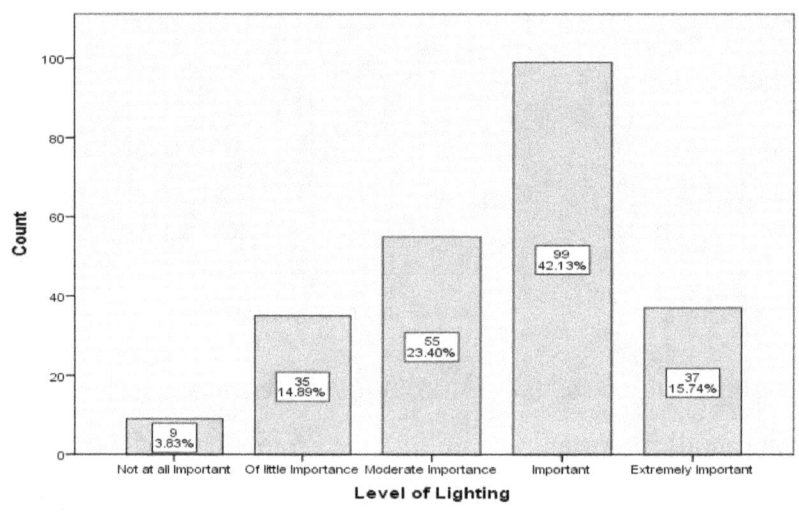

The table given above reflects that 3.83 % of the customers consider the attribute Level of Lighting of the Shopping Centre as not at all important and 14.89 % of the customers consider as of little importance while 23.4 % of the customers have graded as of moderate Importance. 42.13 % customers have graded important to the attribute Level of Lighting of the Shopping Centre while 15.74 % consider this attribute as extremely important.

It can be interpreted that around 57 % of the customers feel that level of lighting at the shop as an important factor deciding their purchase while remaining 43 % of the respondents do not consider lighting level as an important factor.

It can hence be concluded that level of lighting is a moderate factor in the minds of customers.

TABLE No: 5.2.51

Crowd Level experienced by the Respondents

Crowd Level	Frequency	Percent	Valid Percent	Cumulative Percent

Valid	Not at all Important	13	5.5	5.5	5.5
	Of little Importance	39	16.6	16.6	22.1
	Moderate Importance	76	32.3	32.3	54.5
	Important	81	34.5	34.5	88.9
	Extremely Important	26	11.1	11.1	100.0
	Total	**235**	**100.0**	**100.0**	

Source: Field Survey 2012

GRAPH No: 5.2.51

Crowd Level experienced by the Respondents

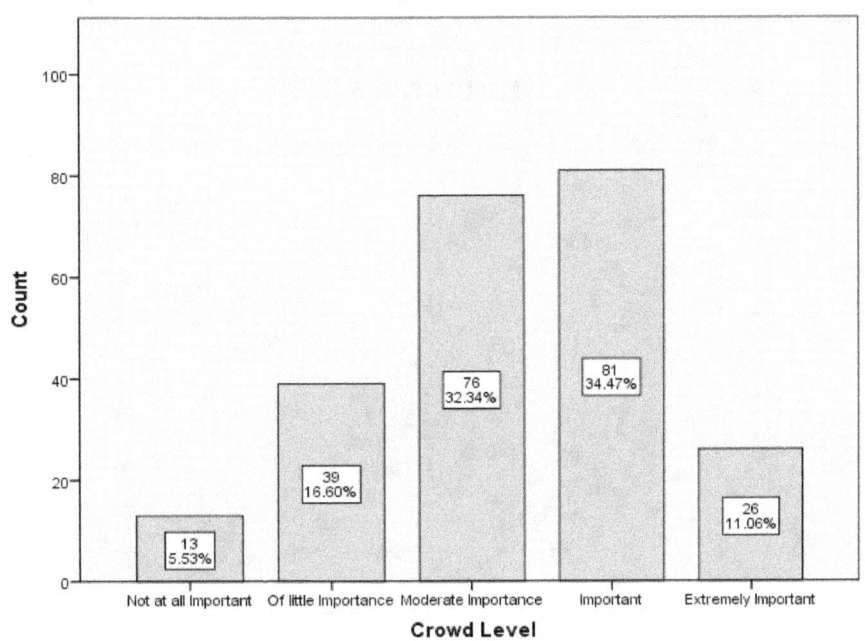

The above graph shows that 5.53 % of the customers consider crowd level as not at all important attribute, 16.60 % customers consider this as of little importance and 32.34 % of the customers have graded as of moderate Importance. 34.47 % customers have graded important to the attribute crowd level of the Shopping Centre while 11.06 % of the customers consider this attribute as extremely important.

It can be inferred that approximately 45 % of the customers feel crowd level as an important factor while remaining 55 % does not consider it of much importance.

It can be concluded that Crowd level attribute of the shopping centre is important as well as of moderate importance to the customers buying in the small retail shops.

TABLE No: 5.2.52

Level of Spaciousness experienced by the Respondents

	Level of Spaciousness	Frequency	Percent	Valid Percent	Cumulative Percent
Valid	Not at all Important	4	1.7	1.7	1.7
	Of little Importance	35	14.9	14.9	16.6
	Moderate Importance	71	30.2	30.2	46.8
	Important	90	38.3	38.3	85.1
	Extremely Important	35	14.9	14.9	100.0
	Total	235	100.0	100.0	

Source: Field Survey 2012

GRAPH No: 5.2.52

Level of Spaciousness experienced by the Respondents

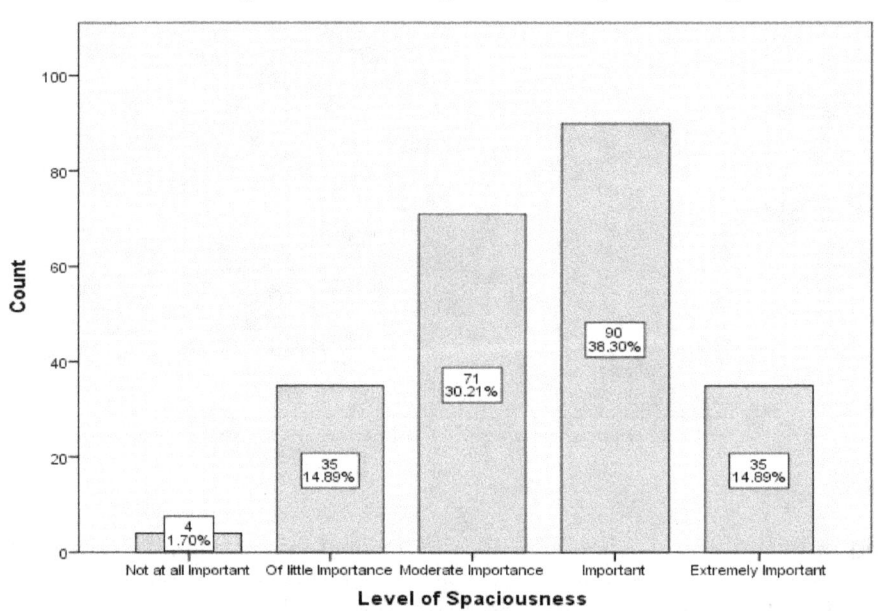

Above graph indicates that 1.70 % of the customers are of the opinion that level of spaciousness is not at all important, 14.89 % customers say that this attribute is of little importance. 30.21 % of the customers have graded Level of Spaciousness as of moderate Importance and 38.30 % customers have graded important to the attribute Level of Spaciousness of the Shopping Centre. While, 14.89 % of the customers have graded this attribute as extremely important.

It can be interpreted that level of spaciousness is considered to be an important factor around 52 % of the customers out of which some give it more importance.

Thus it can be concluded that level of spaciousness is an important attribute for the customers visiting small retail houses.

It is suggested to the retailers to pay attention to this fact and try to keep as much as empty space as possible for making the purchase process more easier for the customers.

TABLE No: 5.2.53
Mode of Payment experienced by the Respondents

	Mode of Payment	Frequency	Percent	Valid Percent	Cumulative Percent
Valid	Not at all Important	4	1.7	1.7	1.7
	Of little Importance	24	10.2	10.2	11.9
	Moderate Importance	55	23.4	23.4	35.3
	Important	115	48.9	48.9	84.3
	Extremely Important	37	15.7	15.7	100.0
	Total	235	100.0	100.0	

Source: Field Survey 2012

GRAPH No: 5.2.53

Mode of Payment experienced by the Respondents

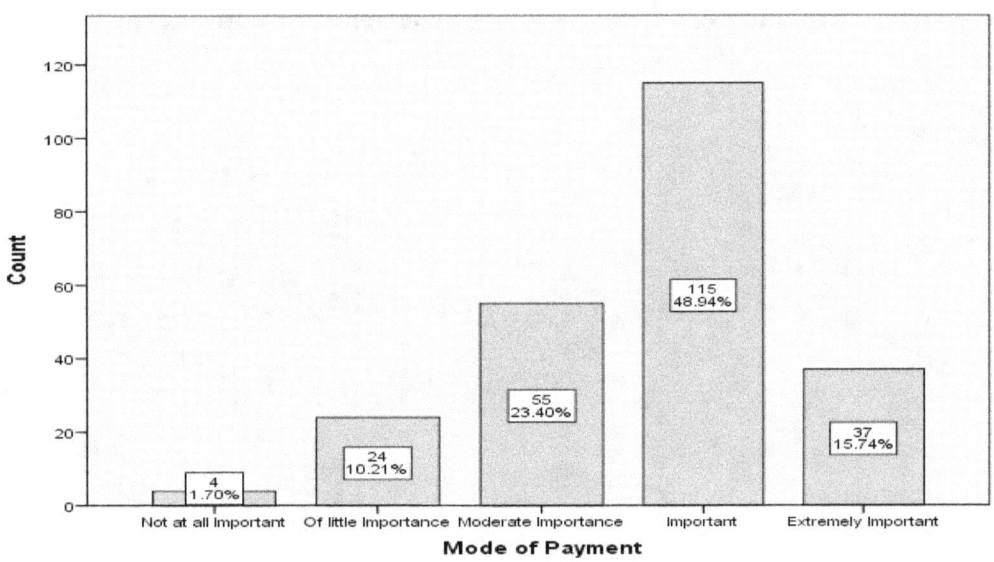

The graph given above indicates that 1.70 % of the customers are of the opinion that mode of payment attribute is not at all important and 10.21 % of the customers say that this factor is of little importance. While, 23.40 % of the customers have graded as of moderate Importance, 48.94 % customers have graded important to the attribute mode of payment of the Shopping Centre. Also, 15.74 % of the customers are saying this attribute is extremely important. It can hence be seen that 63 % of the customers feel that mode of payment is an important factor. It can be concluded that a majority of customers feel that their decisions regarding the choice of shop depends a lot on the mode of payment. It is quite obvious for this to happen as customer's now-a-days want fast service from the retailer. So, quick service of money transfer in the form of mode of payment is an important attribute noted here.

TABLE No: 5.2.54
Opening & Closing Timing experienced by the Respondents

	Opening & Closing Timing	Frequency	Percent	Valid Percent	Cumulative Percent
Valid	Not at all Important	2	.9	.9	.9
	Of little Importance	23	9.8	9.8	10.6
	Moderate Importance	18	7.7	7.7	18.3
	Important	126	53.6	53.6	71.9
	Extremely Important	66	28.1	28.1	100.0
	Total	235	100.0	100.0	

Source: Field Survey 2012

GRAPH No: 5.2.54
Opening & Closing Timing experienced by the Respondents

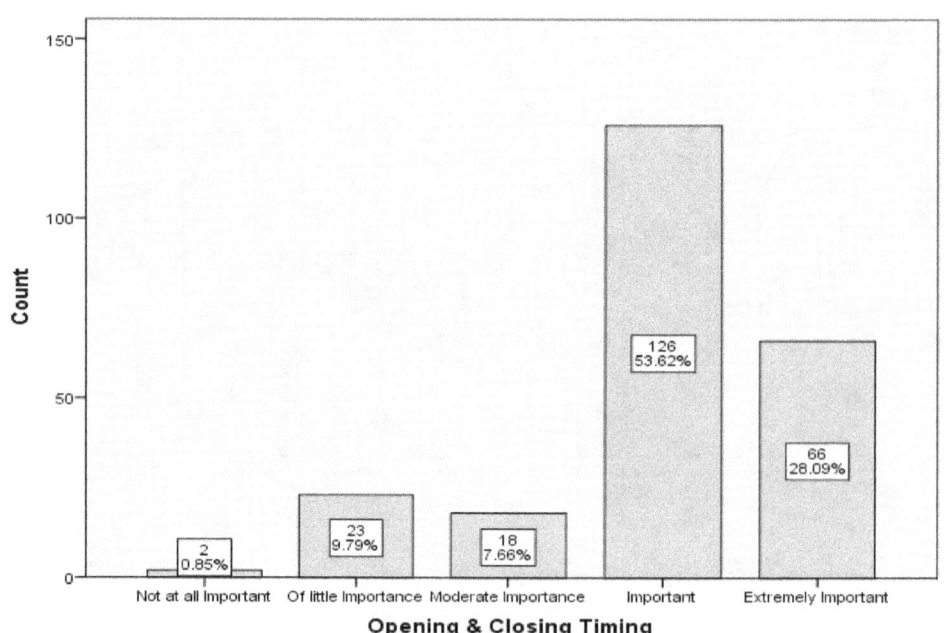

Above graph indicates that only 0.85 % of the customers are of the opinion that Opening & Closing Timing of the Shopping Centre is not at all important, 9.79 % of the customers say that this attribute is of little importance and 7.66 % of the customers say that Opening & Closing Timing of the Shopping Centre is of moderate importance. 53.62 % customers have graded important to the attribute opening & closing Timing of the Shopping Centre while 28.09 % of the customers have graded as of extremely Importance. It can be strongly noted here that around 81 % of the customers feel that their purchase and choice depends on the opening and closing timings of the shop.

Thus it can be concluded that opening & Closing Timing of the retail shop is a very important attribute to the customers. Retail shopkeepers have to take into consideration this aspect and lengthen the working hours of the shop.

TABLE No: 5.2.55
Choice of goods experienced by the Respondents

Choice of goods		Frequency	Percent	Valid Percent	Cumulative Percent
Valid	Not at all Important	12	5.1	5.1	5.1
	Of little Importance	14	6.0	6.0	11.1
	Moderate Importance	48	20.4	20.4	31.5
	Important	85	36.2	36.2	67.7
	Extremely Important	76	32.3	32.3	100.0
	Total	235	100.0	100.0	

Source: Field Survey 2012

GRAPH No: 5.2.55
Choice of goods experienced by the Respondents

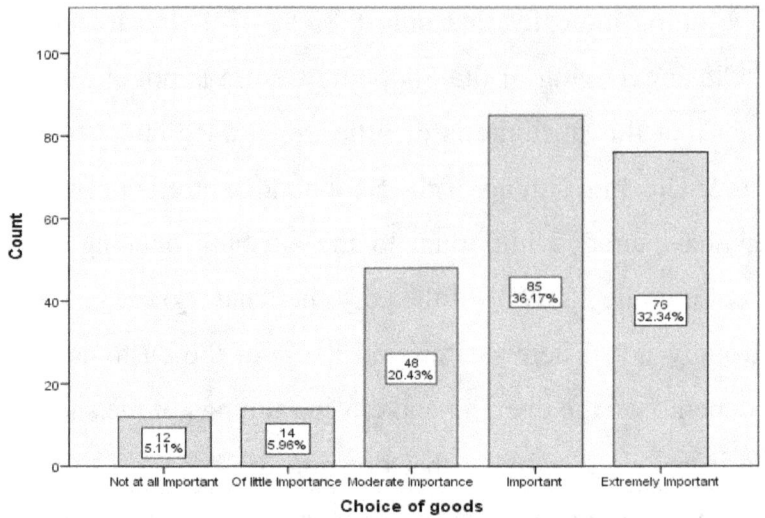

The above graph indicates that 5.11 % of the customers are of the opinion that the choice of goods is not at all important factor and 5.96 % of the customers are of the opinion that choice of goods is of little importance. While, 20.43 % of the customers are of the opinion that the choice of goods at the shopping centre are of moderate importance. 36.17 % customers have graded important to the attribute choice of goods of the Shopping Centre while 32.34 % of the customers have graded as extremely important. Around 69 % of the respondents are of the opinion that choice of goods available at the retail house is an important factor in their decision making. It can be concluded that the choice of goods or the brands available in the shop carries a lot of weight age to the customers. They will be attracted towards the shop only if the shopkeeper stacks the products of the customer's choice.

TABLE No: 5.2.56
Reputation of the Shop experienced by the Respondents

	Reputation of the Shop	Frequency	Percent	Valid Percent	Cumulative Percent
Valid	Not at all Important	5	2.1	2.1	2.1
	Of little Importance	17	7.2	7.2	9.4
	Moderate Importance	42	17.9	17.9	27.2
	Important	109	46.4	46.4	73.6
	Extremely Important	62	26.4	26.4	100.0
	Total	235	100.0	100.0	

Source: Field Survey 2012

GRAPH No: 5.2.56

Reputation of the Shop experienced by the Respondents

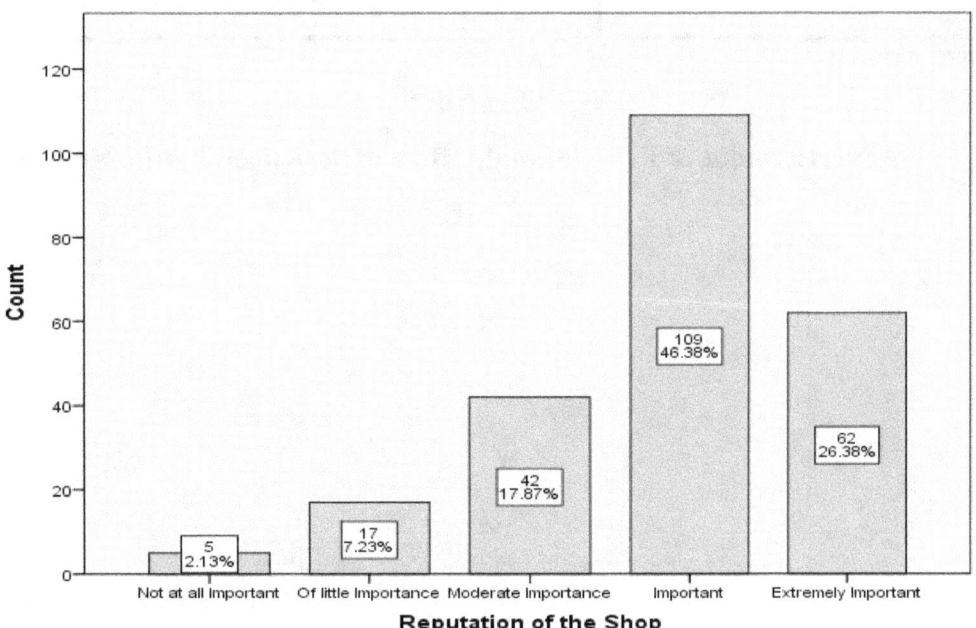

The above graph indicates that 2.13 % of the customers are of the opinion that the attribute Reputation of the shop is not at all important and 7.23 % of the customers consider this attribute as of little importance. While, 17.87 % of the customers have said that reputation of the Shopping Centre is of moderate importance. Also, 46.38 % customers have graded important to the attribute Reputation of the shop while 26.38 % of the customers have graded as Extremely Important. It can be interpreted that approximately 72 % of the respondents feel that they feel reputation of the shop to be an important aspect in deciding the shopping centre.

Hence it can be concluded that reputation of the shop is very important. The customers who shop in the same shop on daily basis are concerned about the reputation of the shop.

TABLE No: 5.2.57

Advertisement & Promotional Offers experienced by the Respondents

Advertisement & Promotional Offers		Frequency	Percent	Valid Percent	Cumulative Percent
Valid	Not at all Important	8	3.4	3.4	3.4
	Of little Importance	23	9.8	9.8	13.2
	Moderate Importance	42	17.9	17.9	31.1
	Important	111	47.2	47.2	78.3

| | Extremely Important | 51 | 21.7 | 21.7 | 100.0 |
| | Total | 235 | 100.0 | 100.0 | |

Source: Field Survey 2012

GRAPH No: 5.2.57

Advertisement & Promotional Offers experienced by the Respondents

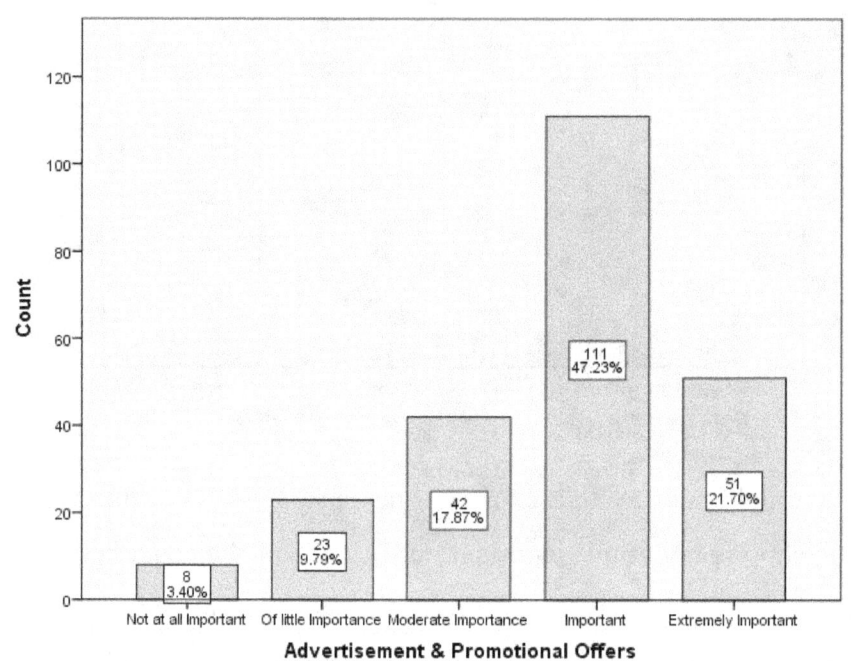

The above graph indicates that 3.40 % of the customers consider the attribute Advertisement & Promotional Offers of the Shopping Centre as not at all important and 9.79 % customers think that this attribute is of little importance. While, 17.87 % of customers say that Advertisement & Promotional Offers at the shopping centre is of moderate Importance. Also, 47.23 % customers have graded important to the attribute Advertisement & Promotional Offers of the Shopping Centre while 21.70 % of the customers have graded as extremely important.

It can be interpreted that 69 % respondents feel that advertisements and the promotional offers play an important role in attracting them towards the shopping centre.

We can conclude that Customers are attracted towards the various schemes, advertisements and promotions offered by the shop.

TABLE No: 5.2.58

Credit Facility experienced by the Respondents

| Credit Facility | Frequency | Percent | Valid Percent | Cumulative Percent |

Valid	Not at all Important	11	4.7	4.7	4.7
	Of little Importance	36	15.3	15.3	20.0
	Moderate Importance	48	20.4	20.4	40.4
	Important	87	37.0	37.0	77.4
	Extremely Important	53	22.6	22.6	100.0
	Total	**235**	**100.0**	**100.0**	

Source: Field Survey 2012

GRAPH No: 5.2.58

Credit Facility experienced by the Respondents

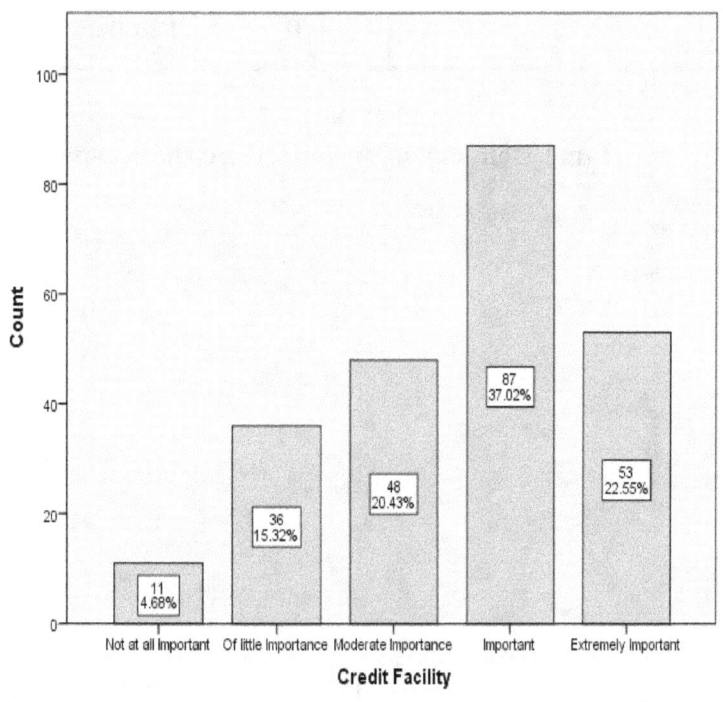

The table given above graph indicates that 4.68 % of customers have graded the attribute credit facility as not at all important and 15.32 % of the customers have graded as of little importance. While, 20.43 % of the customers have graded credit facility given by the shop as of moderate Importance. 37.02 % customers have graded important to the attribute Credit facility of the Shopping Centre and 22.55 % of the customers have graded as extremely important. It can be observed that around 60% of the respondents are of view that the credit facility provided by the shopkeeper plays an important role in their choice of shopping centre. Customers ranging from various income group approach the small retail shops, Hence they expect credit facility from the shopkeeper. It is suggested to the shopkeepers that they should consider providing goods on credit as the customers feel that it is important for them.

TABLE No: 5.2.59
Home Delivery experienced by the Respondents

Home Delivery		Frequency	Percent	Valid Percent	Cumulative Percent
Valid	Not at all Important	17	7.2	7.2	7.2
	Of little Importance	28	11.9	11.9	19.1
	Moderate Importance	48	20.4	20.4	39.6
	Important	97	41.3	41.3	80.9
	Extremely Important	45	19.1	19.1	100.0
	Total	235	100.0	100.0	

Source: Field Survey 2012

GRAPH No: 5.2.59
Home Delivery experienced by the Respondents

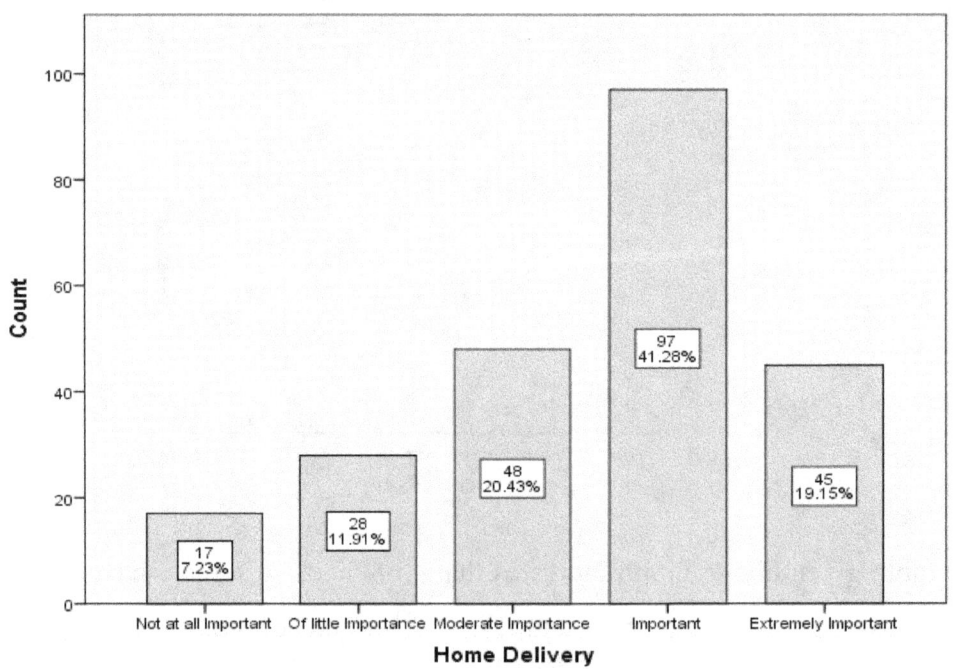

Above graph indicates that 7.23 % of the customers have graded the attribute Home delivery as not at all important and 11.91 have graded as of little importance. While 20.43 % of the customers have graded as of moderate Importance. Also, 41.28 % customers have graded important to the attribute Home delivery of the Shopping Centre and 19.15 % customers have rated as extremely important. It can be concluded that the customers would be happy if home delivery service is made available by the shopkeeper as here around 60 % of them have rated it as the important service attribute.

TABLE No: 5.2.60

Display of Goods experienced by the Respondents

Display of Goods		Frequency	Percent	Valid Percent	Cumulative Percent
Valid	Not at all Important	7	3.0	3.0	3.0
	Of little Importance	21	8.9	8.9	11.9
	Moderate Importance	48	20.4	20.4	32.3
	Important	111	47.2	47.2	79.6
	Extremely Important	48	20.4	20.4	100.0
	Total	235	100.0	100.0	

Source: Field Survey 2012

GRAPH No: 5.2.60

Display of Goods experienced by the Respondents

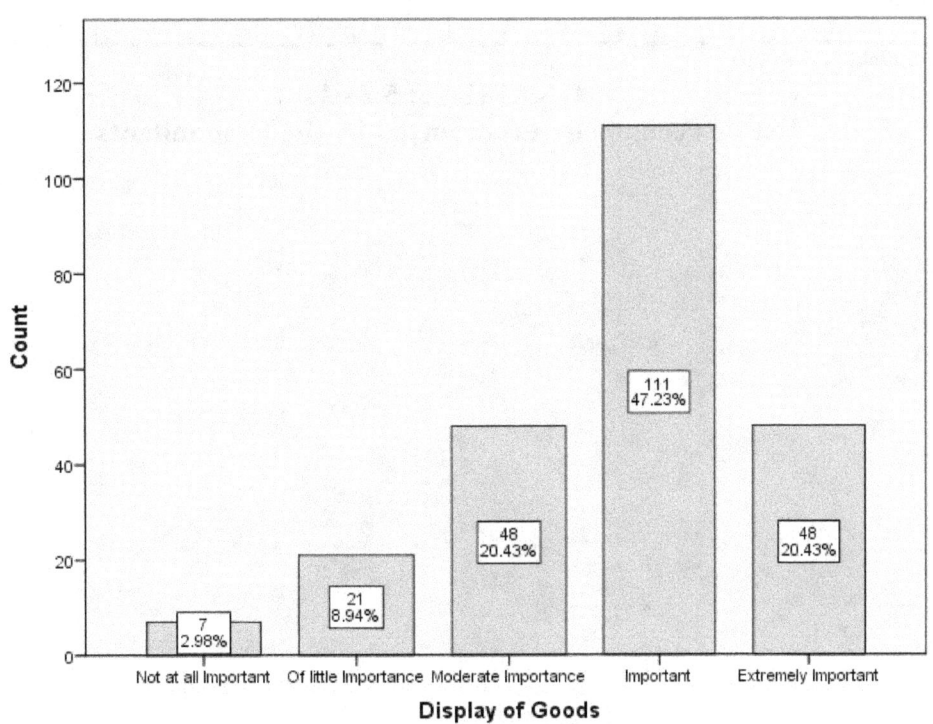

The graph given above indicates that 2.98 % of the customers have graded display of goods as not at all important and 8.94 % customers have graded as of little importance. While 20 % of the customers have graded as of moderate Importance and 47.23 % customers have graded important to the attribute Display of goods of the Shopping Centre. Also, 20 % customers have rated as extremely important to the attribute Display of goods of the Shopping Centre. It can be concluded that approximately 67 % of the respondents feel it is important to have an attractive display of goods at the shop as it makes it more attractive and impulsive. Hence, display of goods is an important shopping attribute where the shopkeeper has to concentrate upon.

TABLE No: 5.2.61
Use of Technology experienced by the Respondents

	Use of Technology	Frequency	Percent	Valid Percent	Cumulative Percent
Valid	Not at all Important	2	.9	.9	.9
	Of little Importance	23	9.8	9.8	10.6
	Moderate Importance	58	24.7	24.7	35.3
	Important	90	38.3	38.3	73.6
	Extremely Important	62	26.4	26.4	100.0
	Total	235	100.0	100.0	

Source: Field Survey 2012

GRAPH No: 5.2.61
Use of Technology experienced by the Respondents

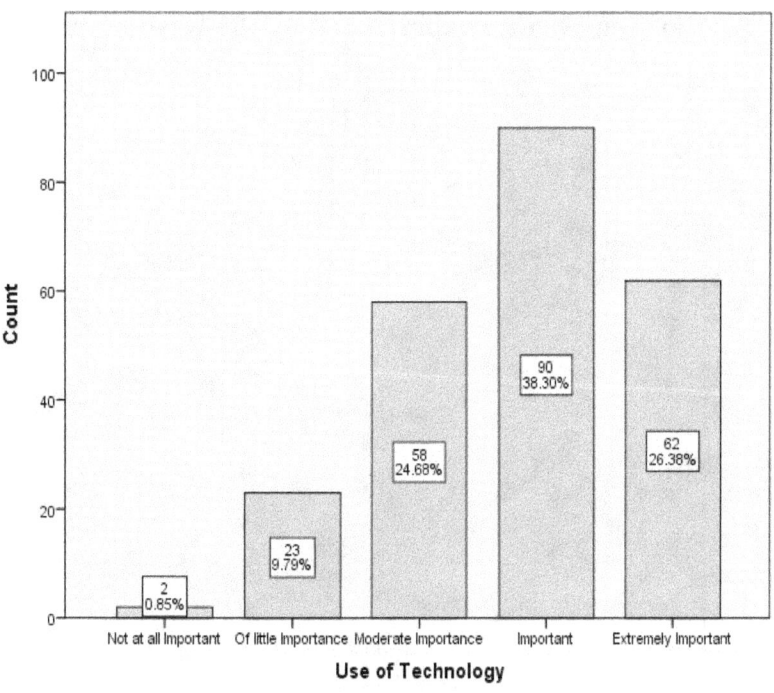

Above graph reflects that 0.85 % of customers rated Use of Technology as not at all important and 9.79 % have rated as of little importance. Also 24.68 % consider this attribute as of moderate Importance and 38.30 % customers have graded important to the attribute use of technology by the Shopping Centre while 26.38 % of the customers have graded as extremely important. It can be interpreted that around 64 % of the respondents feel use of technology to be an important factor for making their purchase easier. It can be concluded that customers prefer use of technology as one of the important attribute so shop owners need to concentrate upon this aspect as well.

TABLE No: 5.2.62
Parking Facility experienced by the Respondents

Parking Facility		Frequency	Percent	Valid Percent	Cumulative Percent
Valid	Not at all Important	9	3.8	3.8	3.8
	Of little Importance	16	6.8	6.8	10.6
	Moderate Importance	46	19.6	19.6	30.2
	Important	101	43.0	43.0	73.2
	Extremely Important	63	26.8	26.8	100.0
	Total	**235**	**100.0**	**100.0**	

Source: Field Survey 2012

GRAPH No: 5.2.62

Parking Facility experienced by the Respondents

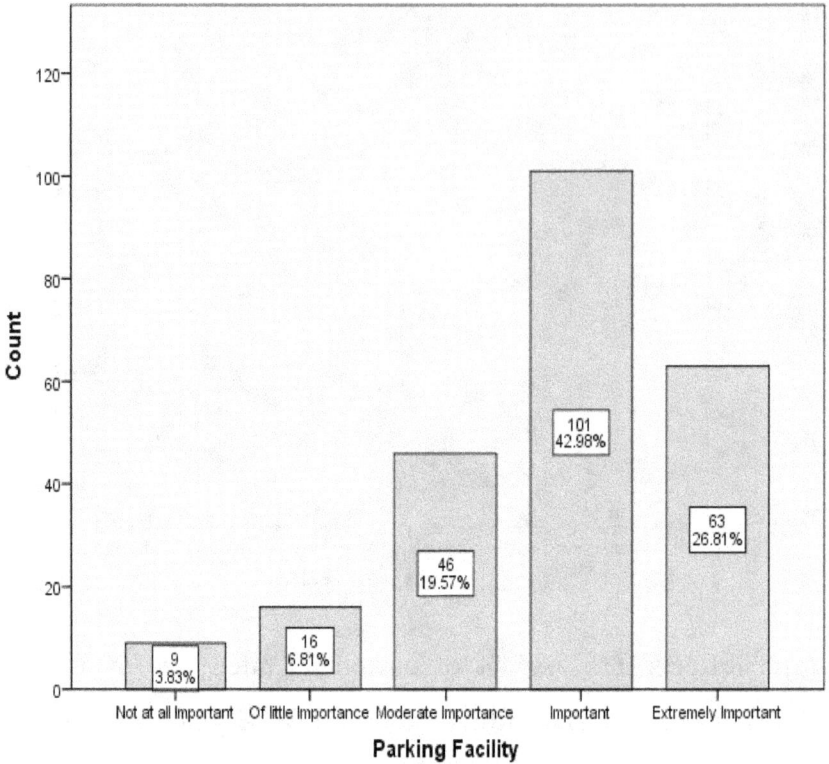

Above graph indicates that 3.83 % of the customers have rated the attribute parking facility as not at all important. Also 6.81 % of customers have rated this attribute as of little importance and 19.57 % are of the opinion that parking facility is of moderate Importance. 42.98 % customers have graded important to the attribute parking facility of the Shopping Centre while 26.81 % of the customers have graded as extremely important. It can be interpreted that around 68 % of the respondents feel that parking facility is an important aspect in their decision regarding the shopping centre. Hence it is suggested that shop owners should see that enough parking area is allotted for the customers visiting the shop.

2. Findings from the customer's lens

It is found highest percentage of customers visiting small retailers lie in the age group of 15-25 followed by the customers of age group 25 -35. It can also be noted that 80% of the customers are in the age group of 15 – 45. This is clearly reflecting that the young generation is mostly visiting the small retailers. It also reinforces the fact that India is a country of youth with an average of 15 – 45 years of age group.

1. Majority of the actual customers who purchase is male. The decision makers are males even when it comes to basic items like grocery. A good sign which is visible is that in concern to decision making the percentage of females is also slowly on an increasing trend.
2. It can be interpreted that majority of the respondents who are buying grocery from small retail shops are from the rural background. Also, it is observed by the researcher that the size of the rural population is growing because of the agricultural income growth in rural part of Kolhapur. The rural market is definitely an opportunity for retailers with an innovative retail proposition.

3. It is evident that majority of customers visiting small retail shop are educated i.e. they have completed their graduation. Also, 32.3 % of the respondents are post graduate. Also it is found that the target customers are from different occupations. Majority of the customers are service people followed by students.
4. It can easily be interpreted that the average monthly family income of the customers is ranging from Rs. 5,000/- to Rs. 30,000/- followed by monthly family income of Rs. 30,000/- – Rs. 45,000/-.Also a large amount of customers are spending Rs. 2000/- – Rs. 7000/- on purchasing grocery from the small retail houses.
5. It is observed that 78.72 % of the customers who visit the small retail shops are having their own vehicle while 21.28 % of the respondents do not possess any vehicle. It can be observed that majority of the respondents visit the small retailers on their vehicles. Also there is a constant flow of the customers to shop the whole of the month. We cannot say that the customers are visiting only during any specific period like weekdays or beginning of the month.
6. Majority of the respondents are having no complaints regarding the availability of the items in the small retail shops.
7. It is found that small retailers are not much concerned about stocking branded products. Majority of the customers i.e. approximately 75 % are having a strong feeling that they are not getting the branded products at the small retailers. Hence it is necessary that small retail shoppers have to concentrate on making the branded products available on time.
8. It is found that approximately 50 % of the respondents are always going to the small retail shops for purchase of household items while remaining 50 % are not so much interested in the household items available at the small retail shops.
9. It is found that 51.06 % of the respondents visiting the small retail houses are satisfied with the quality of customer service while 10.21 % of the respondents visiting the small retail houses are highly satisfied with the services. It is also found that around 62 % of the respondents show a good satisfaction level regarding the quality of services provided by the small retailers.
10. Approximately 40% of the respondents are satisfied with the security arrangements of the small retail shops. But the tables given before had shown that a large majority of customers are satisfied with their shopping experience at the small retail shops.

11. Almost 50% of the customers show their satisfaction towards the prices of the products being comparatively lower than the near by shops in the vicinity. It can thus be construed that less than 50 % of the respondents are satisfied with the emotionality aspect in the buying motive. This shows that the respondents are not purchasing on the emotional terms.
12. Only 40 % of the respondents are satisfied with the crowd level at the small retail houses from where they do their purchase and remaining 60 % of the respondents feel that the shops are crowded and thus they are not satisfied. Hence we can say that crowd is also rated as an important factor for shopping experience by the customer.
13. It is found that around 52 % of the respondents are satisfied with the level of space available at the small retail houses while the remaining 47 % of the respondents do not feel so.
14. It is observed that around 77 % of the respondents visiting the small retail houses of Kolhapur city are satisfied with the opening and closing timings of the shops. It is also construed that around 73 % of the respondents are satisfied with the choice of goods available at the small retail shops while 27 % of them are dissatisfied.
15. It can be interpreted that 66 % of the customers visiting the small retail houses are satisfied with the reputation of the shop while 34 % of the customers are not satisfied.
16. It is found that a majority of the customers i.e. around 66 % are satisfied with the advertisement and promotional offers by the small retail shops.
17. Around 54 % of the customers are satisfied with credit facility while 46 % of them are not satisfied. We know that in business the policy of most of the shopkeepers is that of "NO CREDIT". But when it comes to small kirana shops of Kolhapur city we find that the customers generally look for as per need shopping and monthly billing
18. Only 50 % of the respondents visiting the small retail houses are satisfied with the home delivery services provided by the small retailers which means that the shopkeepers have to go a long way to satisfy the remaining 50 % of the customers visiting the small retail houses.
19. It is found that 65 % of the respondents visiting the small retail houses are satisfied with the display of goods done at the shop by the shopkeepers. It can also be seen that 35% of

the respondents reflect dissatisfaction with the display. Also 55 % of the respondents visiting the small retail houses are satisfied with the use of technology.

20. It can be interpreted that around 63 % of the respondents visiting the small retail houses are satisfied with the parking facility available at the small retail shops.

3 Findings for Shopkeepers

The number of shops chosen were 90 in number

1. A good majority of the shops have an inventory room available with them. It is found that a majority of retailers have their inventory room in near vicinity while around one-third of them have their inventory room away from shop.
2. It is found that more than 50% of the shopkeepers try to make the product available immediately and a very small percentage of shopkeepers say it is not available. Also maximum percentage of the shopkeepers place their order weekly. It is also found that majority of customers decide their order quantity on the basis of judgment.
3. Around 50% of the shopkeepers use a judicious mix of both cash and credit for purchasing the inventory.
4. It is found that around 90 % of the shopkeepers get Credit facilities while remaining 10% of the shopkeepers do not get Credit facilities. Also around 60% of the shopkeepers are satisfied to a great extent with the credit facilities provided by the companies.
5. It is found that around 67 % of the shopkeepers are satisfied regarding replacement of goods getting defective in the transit. Also 71% of the shopkeepers are satisfied with the POP display sent by the company. Also almost all the shopkeepers are satisfied with the financial share of the company in the promotional budget of the shop.

4.Suggestions for Customers

1. It is suggested to the retailers that the target customer largely lies around 15- 45 years and hence their strategies should be designed so as to attract the tastes and preferences of this lot of customers. Also, the segment to be targeted in terms of age bar is mixed but largely above 15 years.
2. It is suggested to the large retail shop owners that as seen from the above table and graph more attention is to be given to the women buyers as well, as they seem to be on an increasing trend in concern with the decision making.

3. It is suggested to the small retailers that they should target rural customers by giving them attractive facilities such as credit facilities, free home delivery, availability of products in small quantity etc.
4. It is suggested that percentage of married customers is only slightly higher than the unmarried ones which indicates the requirements of married and unmarried people should be equally being catered by the small retailers.
5. It is suggested to the small retailers that a family with 3 – 5 number of members is their target. Simultaneously they should take sincere efforts to attract small families also. Attractive schemes, discount offers on first come basis, gifts for children like toffees, small toys etc. can be considered.
6. It is suggested to the retailers that they should think twice before giving false offers or schemes to the customer. If they will do this then they will definitely lose their customers in their long run.
7. It is suggested that considering the shortage of time with the businessmen orders on phone can be taken, home delivery as per their convenient time should be introduced. Opening and closing timings may also be varied as per their spare time.
8. It is suggested to the retailers that they should try to maintain this trust to retain the customers and to attract the new ones.
9. It is suggested to also small retail shopkeepers have to see to it that the parking place is clean enough with a security guards appointed on duty to take care of the vehicles. The parking area can be made use of by flashing hoardings of new arrivals in the shops and making the place more attractive.
10. It is suggested to arrange for a comfortable Two Wheeler parking area in and around the small retail houses.
11. It is suggested to the retailers that they should understand the fact that Kolhapur district is getting urbanized at a very fast pace. The process of globalization has created a strong awareness in the mind of consumers regarding the various brands available for a small product like pencil also. They should keep branded products also in stock so as to retain the customers with them.
12. It is suggested to the small retail shopkeepers to concentrate on window dressing of the shop to increase the number of footfall in the shop.

13. It is suggested that the shopkeepers should take care that they should keep items other than household in which the customers are interested. They should keep stock of all types of items / products at their shops.
14. It is suggested that shopkeepers should concentrate on the quality of grocery items being bought by the customers and should also take care that they are always available whenever the customer demands for them.
15. It is suggested to the shopkeepers that though 62% of the respondents are satisfied with them but simultaneously it cannot be neglected that 38 % is not a small number of customers. They should understand the requirements of these customers also by talking to them or asking their expectations and try to take sincere efforts to satisfy them
16. It is suggested that Customers visiting the small retail houses are happy with the surroundings and all the items in the shop should be kept clean.
17. It is suggested to the shopkeepers to retain the quality of products and to make it more better by keeping more variety of brands to attract customers to their shops. It can be concluded that the small retailers are taking lot of efforts to maintain and upgrade the quality of products available at their shops. They have to compete with the large retailers for sustaining in this competition hence sincere efforts are required. The brands known to the customers and required by the customers should be always available. The grocery items should be clean and hygienically kept with product price tags on them.

5. Suggestions for Shopkeepers

1. It is suggested to the small retailers that the inventory room should be located near the shop only because it will take time to get the things from the inventory room and the customer will have to wait till then. In such a case there are lot many chances that the customers will switch off to a nearby shop.
2. It is suggested to the shopkeepers that they should extend this facility to their customers also so that they will also be satisfied and be retained.
3. It is suggested to the shopkeepers that that they should try to handle the products carefully so as to avoid them from getting defective.
4. It is suggested to the shopkeepers that they should put this display at such a position so as to attract the customers maximum.

6. Implications for Consumers

- The present study suggests that consumers aspiring for entertainment with shopping should visit malls and hyper/supermarkets as these formats provide entertainment facilities to consumers like multiplexes, food courts and background music etc.

- Consumers looking for convenience, comfort and price should favor convenience stores, departmental stores and discount stores.

- Retail formats like malls, hyper/supermarkets are more ideal for young consumers and middle aged consumers with high income group.

- Mature consumers and middle income groups are inclined more towards convenience stores and discount stores.

- Speciality stores should be preferred for buying various shopping goods like jewellery, furniture and clothing, as these stores are highly conscious about quality and offer added product diversity. Consumers will get wide variety of product and a better quality in speciality stores.

- Convenience stores should be preferred for buying various convenience goods like food and grocery, beverages, and confectionaries, generally the low priced goods.

- Consumers should consider a mixture of product and store attributes which are important for them for choosing particular retail format.

7 Implications for Retailers

- Retailers of malls, hyper/supermarkets and speciality stores should focus more upon retention strategies, image improvement strategies and competitive strategies for better management of their business.

- Convenience stores, departmental stores and discount stores need to focus upon promotional and pricing strategies as consumers. Pricing strategy may also help these formats to enhance their sales.

- Retailers need to opt for an appropriate mix of product and store attributes and various goods in their retail outlet. The present study will help them to choose attributes in a retail outlet as per importance given by consumers.

- The current research will facilitate retailers to segment consumers with similar needs and preferences on the basis of age and income. The results of the study depict that young consumers prefer malls more as compared to mature ones. So the retailers of malls need to target young consumers more.

- Now a days, consumers visit emerging retail formats not for shopping only but for entertainment also. So retailers should focus upon entertainment facilities, i.e., opening food court, children play area, background music etc. It will help retailers to keep consumers longer in the store and enjoy shopping.

8. Recommendations for Future Research

Though the present study has covered all the important aspects of retailing from consumers' and retailers' perspective, the survey was limited to Kolhapur City. The future study may cover the other regions of Maharashtra and India to have a comparative view of consumers' and retailers' perspective towards emerging retail formats. Further, case study analysis can be taken up by covering some specific retail formats. It will help to validate the results on the basis of case studies. Some emerging retail formats can be taken as test market and consumers' purchase pattern can be observed from these test markets. Marketing strategies can be varied by retailers in these test centres to see how consumers respond to these strategies.

Opportunities and Challenges of Unorganized Retail sector in India:

Opportunities:

- India's booming economy is a major source of opportunity. It is the third largest in the world in terms of purchasing power. India is the second fastest growing major economy in the world.
- India's huge population has a per capita income of Rs 44,345.

- The proportionate increase in spending with earnings is another source of opportunity.
- With the Indian economy now expected to grow at over 8% and with average salary hikes of about 15%, manufacturers and retailers of consumer goods and services can expect a major boost in consumption.
- The Demography Dynamics are also favourable as approximately 60 per cent of Indian population is below the age of 30.
- Increasing instances of Double Incomes in most families coupled with the rise in spending power.
- Increased urbanization has led to higher customer density areas thus enabling retailers to use lesser number of stores to target the same number of customers. Aggregation of demand that occurs due to urbanization helps a retailer in reaping the economies of scale.
- With increased automobile penetration and an overall improvement in the transportation infrastructure, covering distances has become easier than before. Now a customer can travel miles to reach a particular shop, if he or she sees value in shopping from a particular location.
- Challenges which are faced by the Indian unorganized retail sector:
- Lack of best practice in inventory management and supply chain management.
- Lack of standardization.
- Stiff competition from organized retail sector.
- Lack of knowledge, skills and training.
- Consumers shifting towards organized retail markets.
- Lack of government policies discouraging the unorganized retailers.
- Lack of capital.
- Others

9. Conclusion:

The purpose of the study is to in depth understanding of unorganized retail sector in India. In that way, now a day's Indian consumers are showing rapid changes by shifting their buying attitude from unorganized outlets to organized outlets. In the emerging Indian retail environment, this study has brought insights into importance of unorganized retail sector in India and this will thus help unorganized retailers to frame strategies to face the opportunities and challenges in this sector.

References

1. http://www.academia.edu/1513521/A_Study_on_Increasing_Competitveness_of_Unorganized_Retail_in_India
2. Aluregowda (2013) IOSR Journal of Business and Management (IOSR-JBM)ISSN: 2278-487X. Organized Retail Strategy – A Study at Loyal World Supermarket Volume 7, Issue 1 (Jan. - Feb. 2013), PP 75-80
3. Walsh, Gianfranco and Hennig – Thurau (2001), German Consumer Decision-Making styles, Journal of Consumer Affairs, Volume 35, Issue 1, 73-75, June.
4. Traill, Bruce 2006, The Rapid Rise Of Supermarkets, Development Policy Review, Volume 24, Issue 2, 163-174, March.
5. Bhat and Bowonder (2001), " Innovation as an Enhancer of Brand Personality: Globalization Experience of Titan Industries", Creativity and Innovation Management, Volume 10, Issue1, Page 26-39, March2001.
6. Welsh and Falbe (2006), "An Examination of International Retail Franchising in Emerging Markets", Journal of Small Business Management, Volume 44, Issue1, Page 130-149, January 2006.
7. Engel J.F. Blackwell, R.D, and Miniard P.W. (1990), Consumer Behaviour, (6th ed), Chicao: The Dryden Press.
8. Marteneau, P. (1958, January – February), "The personality of the Retail Sector", Harvard Business Review, 36, pp47-55.

9. Fishbein M. & Ajzen I. 1975; Beliefs, attitude, intension, and behavior : An Introduction to theory and research, Reading, MA: Addison – Wesley.
10. Arrondo E, Berne, C., Mugica, J.M., & Rivera, P. (2002), " Modeling of customer retention in multi-format retailing", The international review of Retail, Distribution and Consumer Research, 12(3), pp 281-296.
11. Ajzen I (1989), " Attitude structure and behavior" in A. R. Pratkanis, S.J. Breckler, and A.G. Greenwalds (Eds.), Attitude structure and function (pp 241-274), Hillsdale, NJ: Lawrence Erlbaum.
12. Shim,S, Eastlick, M. A. Lotz, S.l. & Warrington, P (2001), " An Online Prepurchase intentions model: The role of intention to search", Journal of Retailing 77(3) pp 397-416.
13. Urbany. J.E., Dickson. P>R. and Kalapurakal, R (1996), "Price search in the retail grocery market", "Journel of Marketing, 60(April), pp 91-104.
14. Childers, T. L., Carr, C. L., Peck, J., & Carson, S (2001), " Hedonic and Utilitarian motivations for online retail shopping behavior", Journal of Retailing, 77(4), pp 511-535.
15. Donthu N and Gilliland, A (1996), "The Informercial Shopper", Journal of Advertising Research, 36(2), pp 69-76
16. Reynold, K.E and Beatty S.E (1999b) "A relationship customer typology", Journal of Retailing. 75(4), PP 509 – 523
17. Babin, B.J., Darden, W.R., and Griffin, M (2005), "Work for Fun": Measuring Hedonic and Utilitarian Shopping Value". The Journal of Consumer research, 20(4), pp 644-656.
18. Batra, R and Ahtola, O.T.(1991), "Measuring Hedonic and Utilitarian Sources of Consumer Attitudes", Marketing Letters, 2 (April), pp 159-170.
19. Sinha, P.K (2003), " Shopping Orientation in the evolving Indian Market and Urban Women", Vikalpa, 28 (2) pp 13022., 8 (3) pp 1-6
20. Aggarwal, V. (2008). The Era of Retail Revolution: Contribution to Economy inResearch in Management and Technology. Eds., Aneet and Ramanjeet Singh, Deep and Deep Publications Pvt. Ltd., 429-442.

21. Ali, J., Kapoor, S., and Moorthy, J. (2010). Buying behaviour of consumers for food products in an emerging economy. *British Food Journal,* 112(2), 109-124.

22. Amin, M. (2008). Retailing in India: Assessing the Investment Climate. *India Economy Review,* Sept., 188-197.

23. Anand, K.S., and Sinha, P.K. (2009). Store format choice in an evolving market: role of affect, cognition and involvement. *International Review of Retail, Distribution and Consumer Research,* 19(5), 505-534.

24. Arshad, S.A., and Hisam, M.W. (2007). Issues in Retailing. Eds. Aneet and Ramanjeet Singh, Deep and Deep Publications Pvt. Ltd., 109-118.

25. Bajaj, C, Tuli, R., and Srivastva, N. (2005). Retail Management, Oxford University Press, New Delhi.

26. Barak, B. (1998). Cognitive age: a new multidimensional approach to measuring age identity. *InternationalJournal of Aging and Human Development,* 25(2), 109-127.

27. Benito, O.G., Reyes, C.A.B., Gallego, P.A.M. (2007). Isolating the geo-demographic characterization of retail format choice from the effects of spatial convenience. *Marketing Letters,* 18(1/2), 45-59.

28. Bhardwaj, R.K., and Makkar, U. (2007). Retail Revolution- Emerging Challenges and Issues. *Journal of IMS Group,* 4(2), 9-12.

29. Brennan, D.P., and Lundsten, L. (2000). Impacts of Large Discount Stores on Small US Towns: Reasons for Shopping and Retailer Strategies. *International Journal of Retail & Distribution Management,* 28(45), 155-161.

30. 11.Cn Report. (2008). Retail Scenario in India- Unlimited Opportunity, http: //www. ib ef. org/attachdi splay. aspx? cat_i d=3 7 5 andart_i d=4165.

31. Dalwadi, R., Rathod, H.S., and Patel, A. (2010). Key Retail Store Attributes Determining Consumers' Perceptions: An Empirical Study of

Consumers of Retail Stores Located in Ahmadabad (Gujarat). *SIES Journal of Management,* 7(1), 20-34.

32. Dash, M., and Chandy, S. (2009). A study on the challenges and opportunities faced by organized retail players in Bangalore. http://ssrn.com/abstract=1435218.

33. Erdem, O., Oumlil, A.B., and Tuncalp, S. (1999). Consumer values and the importance of store attributes. *International Journal of Retail & Distribution Management,* 27(4), 137-144.

34. Fam, K.S., Merrilees. B., Richard. J.E., Jozsa. L, Li, Y., and Krisjanous, J, (2011). In-store marketing: a strategic perspective. *Asia Pacific Journal of Marketing and Logistics,* 23(2), 165-176.

35. Fernie, J. (1995). The coming of the fourth wave: new forms of retail out-of-town development. *International Journal of Retail & Distribution Management,* 23(1), 4-11.

36. Fox, E.W., Montgomery, A.L., and Lodish, L.M. (2004). Consumer Shopping and Spending Across Retail Formats. *Journal of Business,* 77(2), S25-S60.

37. Gable, M., Topol, M.T., Lala, V., and Fiorito, S.S. (2008). Differing perceptions of category killers and discount stores. *International Journal of Retail & Distribution Management, 36(10),* 780-811.

38. Ghosh, P., V. Tripathi, and A. Kumar. (2010). Customer expectations of store attributes:A study of organized retail outlets in India. *Journal of Retail & Leisure Property,* 9(1),75-87.

39. Goldman, A. (2001). The transfer of retail formats into developing economies: The example of China. Journal of Retailing, 77(2), 221-242.

40. oswami, P., and Mishra, M.S. (2008). Would Indian consumers move from kirana stores to organized retailers when shopping for groceries? Asia Pacific Journal of

Marketing and Logistics, 21(1), 121-I A3.

41. Goyal, B., and Aggarwal, M. (2009). Organized retailing in India- An empirical study appropriate formats and expected trends. Global journal of Business Research, 3(2), 77-83.

42. Grewal, D., Ailawadi, K.L., Gauri, D., Hall, K., Koppale, P., and Robertson, J.R., (2011). Innovations in Retail Pricing and Promotions. Journal of Retailing 87(1), S43-S52.

43. Grewal, D., Levy, M., and Kumar, V. (2009). Customer Experience Management in Retailing: An Organizing Framework. *Journal of Retailing,* 85(1), 1-14.

44. Gupta, D.D. (2007). Retailing in India and the Role of the Marketing Mix. *European Retail Digest,* 53, 17-20.

45. Gupta, M. (2004). Brand Position of General Store from Consumer's Perspective- A comparative Study on Departmental Store and Traditional Shop. In the Proceedings of the 2004 IPR Conference, Thapar University, Patiala, 25-26.

46. Gupta, S., Jain, k., and Jain, D. (2009). Retention Strategies for Organized Retailers in Semi-Urban Markets. *ICFAI University Journal of Marketing and Management,* VIII (2), 24-37.

47. Guy, CM. (1998) Classifications of retail stores and shopping centres: Some methodological issues. *Geo Journal,* 45, 255-264.

48. Halepete, J., Seshadri, K.V., and Park, S.C. (2008). Wal-Mart in India: a success or failure? *International Journal of Retail & Distribution Management,* 36 (9), 701-713.*Science,* 28(4), 656-673.

49. erpen, E.V., and Pieters, R. (2000). Assortment Variety: Attribute — Versus Product Based. Available at SSRN: http://ssrn.com/abstract=246956.

50. Hino, (2010). Antecedents of supermarket formats' Adoption and usage: A study in context of non-western customers. *Journal of Retailing and Consumer Services,*

17(1), 61-72.

51. ICICI Property Services-Technopak (2007). India Retail Real Estate: The Read Ahead. ICICIProp. Serv. Technopak White Paper, 2007-08.

52. Inani, T. (2007). The Retail Industry: From Myth to Malls. Available at www.managementparadise.com.

53. India Retail Report (2009). The India Retail Story, ww.indiaretailing.com/india-retail-report-2009-detailed-summary.pdf

54. Jackson, P., Aguila, R.P.D., Clarke, I, Hallsworth, A., Kervenoael, R.D., and Kirkup, M. (2006). Retail restructuring and consumer choice 2: understanding consumer choice at the household level. *Environment and Planning A,* 38 (1), *41-61.*

55. Jackson, V., Stoel, S., and Brantley, A. (2011). Mall attributes and shopping value: Differences by gender and generational cohort. *Journal of Retailing and Consumer Services,* 18(5), 1-9.

56. Jacobs, S., Merwe, D.V., Lomard, E., and Kruger, N. (2010). Exploring consumers' preferences with regard to department and specialist food stores. *International Journal of Consumer Studies,* 34, 169-178.

57. Jain, R., and Bagdare, S. (2009). Determinants of Customer Experience in New Format Retail Stores. *Journal of Marketing & Communication,* 5 (2), 34-44.

58. Jasola, M. (2007). Emerging Trends in Retail Sector. *Journal of IMS Group,* 4 (2), 22-28.

59. Jhamb, D., and Kiran, R. (2011). A Strategic Framework for Consumer Preferences towards Emerging Retail Formats. *Journal of Emerging Knowledge on Emerging Markets,* 3, 437-453.

60. Jhamb, D., and Kiran, R. (2012). Emerging Trends of Organized Retailing in India: A Shared Vision of Consumers and Retailers Perspective. *Middle-East Journal of Scientific Research,* 11 (4), 481-490.

61. Jhamb, D., and Kiran, R. (2012). Trendy shopping replacing traditional format preferences. *African Journal of Business Management,* 6(11), 4196-4207.

62. Kamaladevi, B. (2010). Customer Experience Management in Retailing. *Business Intelligence Journal,* 3(1), 37-54.

63. Kaur, P., and Singh, R. (2007). Uncovering retail shopping motives of Indian youth. *Young Consumers,* 8 (2), 128-138.

64. Kearney, A.T. (2010). Expanding opportunities for global retailers", *Global Retail Development Index,* 3M ATK.0610.136.

65. Kim, S.Y., Jung. T.S., Suh, E.H., and Hwang, H.S. (2006). Customer segmentation and strategy development based on customer lifetime value: A case study. Expert Systems with Application, 31, 101-107.

66. Kocas, C, and Bohlmann, J.D. (2008). Segmented Switchers and Retailer Pricing Strategies. *Journal of Marketing,* 72, 124-142.

67. Kokatnur, S.S. (2009). Impact of Supermarkets on Marketing Strategies of Small Stores. *The IUP Journal of Management Research,* VIII (8), 78-90.

68. Kotler, P. (2006). Marketing Management, Prentice Hall of India Private Limited, New Delhi.

69. Kuruvilla, S.J., and Ganguli, J. (2008). Mall development and operations: an Indian perspective. *Journal of Retail & Leisure Property,* 7(3), 204-15.

www.ingramcontent.com/pod-product-compliance
Lightning Source LLC
Chambersburg PA
CBHW081726170526
45167CB00009B/3710